SMO3002361
5.04
£17.00

796.440834
(MaL)

D0537194

WITHDRAWN

WITHDRAWN

WITHDRAWN
ST MARTINS SERVICES LTD

KidDeveloping S®

A Child-Centered Approach to Teaching Gymnastics

Eric Malmberg, EdD
State University of New York at Cortland

Human Kinetics

Library of Congress Cataloging-in-Publication Data

Malmberg, Eric, 1952-
    KiDnastics : a child-centered approach to teaching gymnastics / Eric
Malmberg.
        p. cm.
Includes bibliographical references (p.).
    ISBN 0-7360-3394-7 (Soft cover)
    1. Gymnastics for children. 2. Gymnastics--Study and teaching. I.
Title.
    GV464.5 .M34 2003
    796.44'083'4--dc21

                        2002011828

ISBN: 0-7360-3394-7

Copyright © 2003 by Eric Malmberg

All rights reserved. Except for use in a review, the reproduction or utilization of this work in any form or by any electronic, mechanical, or other means, now known or hereafter invented, including xerography, photocopying, and recording, and in any information storage and retrieval system, is forbidden without the written permission of the publisher.

FlagHouse, Inc. is the registered owner of the trademark KiDnastics and the exclusive supplier of KiDnastics equipment. For information contact FlagHouse, 601 FlagHouse Drive, Hasbrouck Heights, New Jersey 07604, telephone 201-288-7600, facsimile 201-288-7887, e-mail info@flaghouse.com, web site www.flaghouse.com.

Notice: Permission to reproduce the following material is granted to instructors and agencies who have purchased *KiDnastics: A Child-Centered Approach to Teaching Gymnastics:* figures 3.1 through 3.5, 10.3, and the task cards in the appendix. The reproduction of other parts of this book is expressly forbidden by the above copyright notice. Persons or agencies who have not purchased *KiDnastics: A Child-Centered Approach to Teaching Gymnastics* may not reproduce any material.

Acquisitions Editor: Judy Patterson Wright, PhD; **Developmental Editor:** Melissa Feld; **Assistant Editor:** Susan C. Hagan; **Copyeditor:** Jan Feeney; **Proofreader:** Red Inc.; **Graphic Designer:** Robert Reuther; **Graphic Artist:** Kathleen Boudreau-Fuoss; **Photo Manager:** Leslie A. Woodrum; **Cover Designer:** Robert Reuther; **Photographer (cover):** John Paul Endress; **Photographer (interior):** Eric Malmberg; **Art Manager:** Kelly Hendren; **Illustrator:** Roberto Sabas; **Printer:** United Graphics

Printed in the United States of America   10 9 8 7 6 5 4 3 2 1

Human Kinetics
Web site: www.HumanKinetics.com

United States: Human Kinetics
P.O. Box 5076, Champaign, IL 61825-5076
800-747-4457
e-mail: humank@hkusa.com

Canada: Human Kinetics
475 Devonshire Road Unit 100, Windsor, ON N8Y 2L5
800-465-7301 (in Canada only)
e-mail: orders@hkcanada.com

Europe: Human Kinetics
107 Bradford Road, Stanningley, Leeds LS28 6AT, United Kingdom
+44 (0) 113 255 5665
e-mail: hk@hkeurope.com

Australia: Human Kinetics, 57A Price Avenue, Lower Mitcham, South Australia 5062
08 8277 1555
e-mail: liahka@senet.com.au

New Zealand: Human Kinetics
P.O. Box 105-231, Auckland Central
09-523-3462
e-mail: hkp@ihug.co.nz

This book is lovingly dedicated to my wife, Sue.

CONTENTS

ACKNOWLEDGMENTS

There are many people to thank in a project of this magnitude, so I will try to acknowledge in chronological order. First, I must thank my wife, Sue, who is one of the best teachers I know and who was an early sounding board many years ago when we first started to "think out of the box" about gymnastics teaching in school settings. I credit her with first coining the term *KiDnastics* as a way to describe what kids were telling us in their movement and play.

Second, I must thank my colleagues who served with me on the USA Gymnastics Education Sub-Committee: Patty Hacker, Jim Nance, Susan True, and Alan Tilove. The growth, insight, and friendship we all experienced from our "committee years" together had a serious impact on this book. It was easily the most enjoyable, hardest working, and most productive committee on which I have ever served.

I save a very special thank-you for Garland O'Quinn, whose work and good thinking was far ahead of his time. Garland is one of the most remarkable people I have ever met and he certainly helped reshape my thinking about kids and gymnastics. He is an honored colleague, and I am happy to have shared ideas with him over the years. His work seriously influenced this book. I will never forget our early discussions on *environmental manipulation,* a term we collectively coined as a better way to describe a form of progression teaching.

Next, I want to acknowledge my colleagues at SUNY-Cortland, particularly Gary Babjack, who is a virtual idea factory and whose good teaching helps us continue the evolution of KiDnastics as a legitimate pedagogical model for gymnastic teaching. I also want to thank Phyllis McGinley for a career of inspired teaching and Mike Kniffin, Kath Howarth, and Diane Craft for their encouragement over the years. You all helped this book come about. Thanks.

The good folks at Flaghouse, Inc. were so very helpful in not only this project but also in the development of a different, uniquely designed line of KiDnastics equipment—some of which can be seen in the photos of this book. I want to especially thank Doug Liebau for his helpfulness, efficiency, and good thinking in the design of many of the KiDnastics environments we now use. I would also like to thank Sue Schiemer for her outstanding creativity in designing environments and assessments.

I would like to thank my developmental editor, Melissa Feld, who was a sheer pleasure to work with and who made this project a manageable task. Thank you Melissa.

Finally, I would like to thank Larry Thomas, principal at Appleby Elementary School in Marathon, New York for the use of their facilities and of course the kids who so willingly volunteered for the photographs used in this book: Brianna Ackley, Marta and Lucas Malmberg, Taylor Ryan, and Leah and Margaret Thon. They are real KiD-nasts!

HOW TO USE THIS BOOK

The main goal of this book is to communicate and bring to life an instructional model that simplifies the teaching of gymnastics. The distinguishing feature of KiDnastics® lessons is the teacher's use of nontraditional equipment to provide different practice environments. Over the years we have found that workshops have been very successful in providing the visual examples teachers need to link theory to practice. As a result we have attempted to make this book very visual by providing many line drawings and photographs. Once familiar with the major ideas and guiding principles of KiDnastics, teachers should be able to quickly scan the appropriate section or chapter for useful and creative ideas.

Readers should start their KiDnastics journey by reading **part I,** "Understanding KiDnastics." The three chapters of part I explain the major principles of the KiDnastics model, why the model is needed, and how it evolved. Chapter 1, "Rethinking Gymnastics Instruction: How KiDnastics Evolved," emphasizes the notion of KiDnastics as a hybrid model—a rethinking and a simplification of traditional gymnastics teaching. This chapter also introduces the concept of *environmental manipulation* (EM) as well as KiDnastics as a simple three-step approach. Chapter 2, "Environmental Manipulation: An Approach to Skill Development," identifies EM as the major feature of the KiDnastics model and methodically explains the idea through some sample illustrations. Chapter 3, "Teaching and Assessing KiDnastics," further explains the teaching of KiDnastics as a process of *practicing, sequencing,* then *performing.* Figure 3.1 (p. 18) presents the entire KiDnastics model in its most condensed form.

Part II is the section of the book that teachers will most often refer to. It takes the reader through the first step of the KiDnastics approach: practicing environmentally. Chapters 4 through 8 focus on environmental practice ideas for each KiDnastics movement category: rolling, jumping, balancing, vaulting, and hanging and climbing. Each chapter provides detailed KiDnastics practice ideas and variations. Chapters 4 through 8 are similarly structured so that the teacher can easily find examples of environmental practice for any skill or theme listed. In addition, the reader will notice that teaching cues are also provided to help prompt learners. Performance points are also listed to help guide teachers while formally or informally assessing student work.

Part III helps the teacher guide students through the processes of *sequencing* and *performing* (chapter 9). A variety of practice options are presented, particularly the use of illustrated task cards, which allow teachers to present practice tasks more clearly through a visual medium. Chapter 10 helps the teacher organize a culminating event to their instructional unit—a KiDnastics show—by providing organizational ideas, formats, checklists, and sample parental newsletters. Concluding thoughts on KiDnastics are also presented. Teachers should find the appendix particularly useful; this provides numerous task cards that can be used in a variety of ways. The task cards are printed on perforated paper so they can be easily detached. They are presized and ready for reproducing and laminating. The task cards have been grouped by skill category. Consider copying each skill category on different colored paper. This will allow you to locate each skill category more quickly.

PART I

Understanding KiDnastics®

Rethinking Gymnastics Instruction
How KiDnastics® Evolved

It was nearly 20 years ago that I found myself, once again, teaching kids that activity we all loved so dearly—gymnastics. Every day my colleagues and students set up our balance beams, parallel bars, rings, ropes, and a mountain of fold-up mats. We taught and learned traditional gymnastics skills. Like others who taught gymnastics, we also spent much time dragging around heavy gymnastics equipment, worrying about students' safety, and agonizing over skills that Mary and Billy just couldn't quite figure out how to learn. We tried to figure out the forward roll and the backward roll, and many (but not all) even learned a cartwheel and beyond. We used the equipment properly and religiously taught what we believed to be the correct technique for a variety of gymnastics skills. Indeed, our instructional program was solid.

Listening With Our Eyes

Then one day we noticed that a boy and girl took a fold-up mat and began to use it to practice balance beam skills. Having success at doing a cartwheel on this rather wide version of a balance beam, the pair added another mat and began to practice in unison, starting and finishing at the same time. Delighted with their invention, they continued their work and began to use the panel mat blocks in different ways. They rolled up onto them, leapfrogged over them, and jumped off of them. Their work was continuous, creative, and usually in unison. The next day this same pair came to class early to help the instructors set up; they found themselves inventing more sequences with even more elaborate equipment configurations. Other kids followed suit and developed partner sequences of their own—all on whatever equipment they could puzzle together in nontraditional ways. The fun had started, but our gym was a mess! Two days later we observed student-created partner routines 21 skills long! Not bad for three brief practices!

What was it that we were seeing? Their smiles and creative work seemed to be telling us something about the joy of moving and the interplay of movement and the environment. After some discussion, we concluded that this was merely our students' innocent interpretation of gymnastics. In a sense, this was the kids' version of the adult traditional gymnastics, or as one teacher put it, "This is kid-nastics." The activity now had a name!

After continued thought and several years of trial and error, we were convinced that kids understood something adults did not. Weren't kids actually suggesting a whole different approach to teaching gymnastics—a more child-friendly form? What were the principles that framed this "kid-nastics"? These were the driving questions that led to this book. And so for several years we listened with our eyes to the wisdom of children as their movement and joy told us how to rethink the content and method of gymnastics instruction for all children.

Other Gymnastics Models

Over the past 200 years two models have dominated practice in gymnastics instruction: traditional (or artistic gymnastics) and educational gymnastics. Both models have interesting histories but differing philosophies, resulting in differing aims and teaching methods. Fans of each of the models frequently debate the pros and cons of the two approaches.

Traditional Gymnastics

The instructional problems associated with traditional gymnastics are well documented. This well-known form of instruction defines gymnastics as an individual competitive sport with a goal of performing routines on specific apparatus. These apparatus are sometimes called the Olympic apparatus: floor exercise, balance beam, pommel horse, rings, parallel bars, uneven parallel bars, vault, and high bar. Specific skills in the sport are named and assigned a difficulty level (A, B, C, D, E); an emphasis is placed on proper execution of skills, known as form (such as toes pointed, legs together and straight). The dominant teaching method is direct instruction with an emphasis on progression and spotting by a partner or instructor. Safety has long been a concern in traditional gymnastics because students are required to work on apparatus with standardized dimensions. This equipment standardization usually calls for spotters who are able to perform their tasks well. Critics of traditional gymnastics usually cite safety, competition, teacher-centered methods, complexity of movements, and heavy equipment management as instructional problem areas.

Educational Gymnastics

Educational gymnastics is an instructional model developed from educational dance and Laban's effort concepts of time, space, force, and flow. Although Laban never intended his concepts to be used outside the discipline of dance, educational gymnastics gained much support through the 1950s and 1960s and has more recently enjoyed a renaissance of interest. Educational gymnastics uses predominantly child-centered styles of instruction. Teachers often initiate work by posing general movement problems that children can solve in a variety of ways (that is, students are asked to problem solve). Work is usually done individually and sometimes with partners on nontraditional apparatus. The concept of individual choice in solving movement problems is an important part of educational gymnastics. Critics of this model usually contend that educational gymnastics requires much time to develop skill difficulty and requires extensive teacher training for understanding and implementing the concepts involved.

Regardless of which model of gymnastics instruction one prefers, it is more important to recognize that both models have strengths and weaknesses. The wisdom of children revealed how elements of both models could be combined to produce another model—KiDnastics!

A Hybrid Model

KiDnastics is a model that borrows elements from both traditional and educational gymnastics. In a sense, it is a hybrid model, born of the other two. But KiDnastics is more than a simple blending of two instructional modes; a legitimate model must make a unique contribution. Our early "kid-nasts" clearly identified this uniqueness as the changing and manipulation of the practice environment.

Manipulating the Environment

As a model of gymnastics instruction, KiDnastics is unique in that the conceptual focus is on the practice environment and how it can be adapted, changed, or manipulated to produce more efficient student learning. We coined the term *environmental manipulation* (EM) to describe the process. The teacher's primary focus is presenting a task that is first practiced in one environment, then extended through practice in many different environments. In this way student movement repertoire is expanded. Environmental manipulation also allows teachers to provide for individual differences by modifying or reconfiguring the practice environment.

The practice environment serves another function—it shapes movement. As learners travel from one practice environment to another, they adjust their responses to the different settings, thus creating a new variation of the original skill. In this way the new practice environment has extended the learner's movement capability. For example, suppose you wanted to teach a child a simple type of forward roll. You could arrange student practice first down an incline mat until students reach a desired level of control. You could then shape and extend forward rolling practice by providing a variety of rolling environments, such as *up* hills, *over* objects, *under* bungee cords, *through* hula hoops, and so on. In this

way you have manipulated the rolling environment, and the environment has shaped the movements and extended the learners' movement repertoire.

Teachers can further extend students' movement abilities by changing the practice conditions from individual work to work with a partner or in a group. Working with partners in unison is a great way to get students to extend and refine the skills they have acquired.

Increasing Movement Vocabulary

The aim of the KiDnastics model is to expand the learner's movement repertoire, or increase one's movement vocabulary. Just as we expand our verbal vocabulary by learning new words and discovering new uses for words, we can also expand our movement vocabulary by learning new movement skills. KiDnastics teachers seek to develop a wide range of movement capabilities through environmentally manipulated practice. With this approach the emphasis is not on increasing the difficulty of movement but on increasing diversity of the movement's application. For instance, when we teach rolling skills, it is not so important for a child to master the traditional forward roll on a flat mat. A more important aim is for the student to be able to do that forward roll in many different environments. In this way the child becomes a better roller because he can perform the roll in different settings.

Simplifying Instruction: Five Movement Categories

Nearly all forms of gymnastics (traditional, rhythmic, and educational) encompass a great amount of skills and complexity. This complexity usually adversely affects teachers' ease and confidence in teaching gymnastics. The KiDnastics model, however, frames its content around just five movement categories (see figure 1.1). Grouping related skills and themes into a small number of categories greatly simplifies content for teachers.

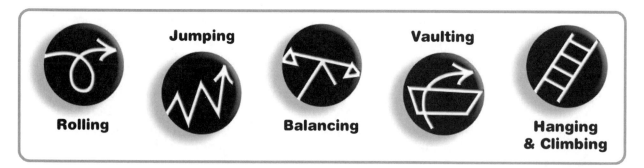

FIGURE 1.1 The development of students' movement vocabulary in each of these five areas is a primary focus in KiDnastics.

In short, the goal of the teacher is to develop students who are good rollers, jumpers, balancers, vaulters, and hangers and climbers (see figure 1.2). See part II, "Practicing Environmentally," for information on helping students develop skills within these categories.

> **A good roller, jumper, balancer, vaulter,
> and hanger and climber can do many different rolls,
> jumps, balances, vaults, and hangs and climbs
> in many different environments!**

FIGURE 1.2   A litmus test for KiDnastics.

A Three-Step Process

After many years of experimentation and countless workshops, we are able to simplify the teaching of KiDnastics into three easy-to-understand steps. Once you select a skill or theme, notice how learning experiences are divided into three levels of progression (figure 1.3). In this way students are led through a process of extension and refinement:

1. Work on single skills in different environments.
2. Link skills together.
3. Perform the skills.

A Three-Step Instructional Process

Get ready! Pick a skill or theme.

- Roll
- Jump
- Balance
- Vault
- Hang and climb

Step 1: Practicing

- Practice single skills or themes in different environments.
- Practice skills alone, then with a partner.

Step 2: Sequencing

- Link skills together *within* and *across* the five movement categories.
- Practice in different environments.
- Practice alone, then with a partner, in groups of three, four, and so on.

Step 3: Performing

- Create, refine, then show your work.
- Work alone or with a partner, in groups of three, four, and so on.

FIGURE 1.3   KiDnastics is as easy as 1, 2, 3!

A Style-Free Model

Because the major focus of KiDnastics is on the manipulation of the practice environment, the model does not dictate exclusive use of one teaching style over another. It has been our observation that KiDnastics has equal appeal with teachers who use child-centered, indirect, and problem-solving styles as well as teachers who favor more direct styles.

Summary

KiDnastics is a simplification and a rethinking of traditional gymnastics. Its emphasis is on the following unique features:

- KiDnastics is a hybrid model of instruction.
- KiDnastics focuses on the environment and manipulation of that environment.
- KiDnastics increases learners' movement vocabulary.
- KiDnastics provides for individual differences.
- KiDnastics frames content around just five movement categories.
- KiDnastics simplifies instruction in three easy steps.
- KiDnastics uses a variety of teaching styles.
- KiDnastics uses safe environments.
- KiDnastics requires little or no spotting.

Environmental Manipulation
An Approach
to Skill Development

The major feature of the KiDnastics model is the manipulation of the practice environment to produce learning outcomes for students. Teachers can use environmental manipulation to focus on two different outcomes:

1. Expand movement vocabulary (general).
2. Shape skills (specific).

Expanding Movement Vocabulary

In most KiDnastics lessons, teachers guide students through the three-step process of *practicing, sequencing,* and *performing.* The first step, practicing, involves the presentation and practice of a skill or task in one particular setting. The learner practices this initial skill or task until she reaches a desired level of control. Then the learner proceeds to practice that same skill or task in a variety of environments. In this way the environment begins to create differences in the original skill (response 1), thus increasing the child's ability to adapt an original response to a variety of settings (see figure 2.1).

If a child is able to do a particular skill or task in one environment, that does not mean he will be able to do it in other environments. Skill or task mastery implies the ability to apply the skill or task to a variety of settings. From this point of view a good shoulder roller is not one who can do the skill in one particular environment, but one who can do shoulder rolls in many different environments. In short, environmental manipulation of practice is used to expand movement vocabulary.

Specific Shaping of Skills

Environmentally manipulated practice not only expands students' movement vocabulary, but it can also shape specific skill outcomes. Many years ago while on a sport-study tour of Soviet Russia, we had the opportunity to visit a Soviet gymnastics research center. We saw a variety of experimental machines and other ingenious contraptions designed to help gymnasts learn the complicated skills of their craft. Primarily what we saw were devices and methodologies that modified or manipulated the environment to make the complex skills simpler. I saw devices to help teach twisting, deep foam landing pits to eliminate landing errors, and even antigravity harnesses that could slow down or speed up rotating gymnasts. These were the most extreme examples of environmental manipulation one could imagine! These environmental manipulations helped coaches to shape their athletes' learning by focusing on skills or parts of skills. The following two specific skill problems illustrate how students can achieve a movement goal through a teacher's deliberate manipulation of the environment (see figures 2.2 and 2.3).

Nontraditional KiDnastics Environments

There are no required KiDnastics equipment or apparatus; this is one of the strong features of the model. Many teachers simply take what equipment they currently have in storage and use it in different ways to create environments that promote rolling, jumping, balancing, vaulting, and hanging and climbing.

Perhaps the most versatile piece of equipment is the standard fold-up (panel) mat. These can be used in many different ways to create different KiDnastics environments. Figure 2.4, a through d, shows a variety of useful panel mat configurations. Panel mats can also be used in combination with other pieces to create different environments for rolling, jumping, balancing, vaulting, and hanging and climbing (see figures 2.5 through 2.8 on pages 14–15). Different environments can promote different kinds of movements. A KiDnastics teacher uses different environments to shape and expand movement vocabulary. Notice how the sloped environments such as the big hill, mountain peak, and valley could promote rolling while the ministairway, the T, and the H provide environments suitable for jumping.

Response 1

Shoulder roll on a flat mat.

FIGURE 2.1 Each environmental variation (1A, 1B, 1C, and so on) provides a different practice environment for the learner.

Response 1A

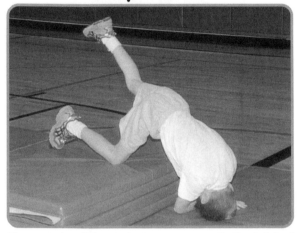

Forward roll from knees on partially folded panel mat.

Response 1B

Shoulder roll down an incline.

Response 1C

Shoulder roll up an incline.

Response 1D

Shoulder roll down from a straddle stand on a low beam.

Movement or skill problem A

Student can roll forward but cannot roll onto feet.

FIGURE 2.2 Environmental manipulation provides solutions to movement and skill problems. All of these environmental solutions can help the student roll to his feet.

Environmental solution A1

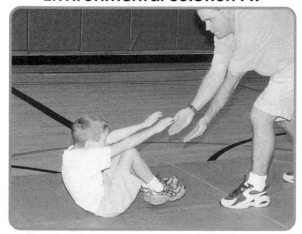

"Gimme 10!" Focus student's attention on reaching forward with the hands.

Environmental solution A2

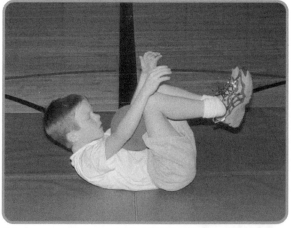

"Squeeze the foam ball!" Rolling with a foam or sock ball between thighs and belly focuses attention on the tucked body position.

Environmental solution A3

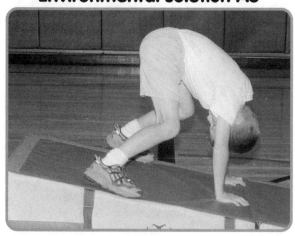

"Down the hill!" Incline increases momentum.

Environmental solution A4

"Use all three environmental manipulations at the same time!" Putting all the solutions together helps the student to roll onto feet.

Movement or skill problem B

Student is inconsistent in recovering from a cartwheel-type movement.

FIGURE 2.3 These environmental solutions can help the learner with cartwheel recovery problems.

Environmental solution B1

"Up the hill!" Cartwheeling up a hill makes the learner kick harder.

Environmental solution B2

"The bungee tunnel." Cartwheeling between two bungee cords focuses attention on linear movement.

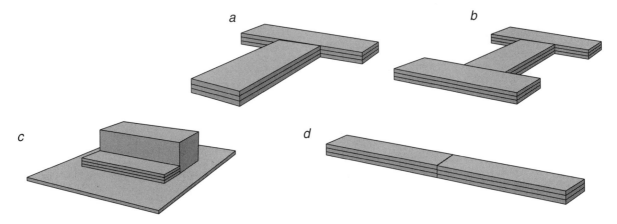

FIGURE 2.4 Panel mats provide versatility in creating KiDnastics environments: the T *(a)*, the H *(b)*, the ministairway *(c)*, and the line *(d)*.

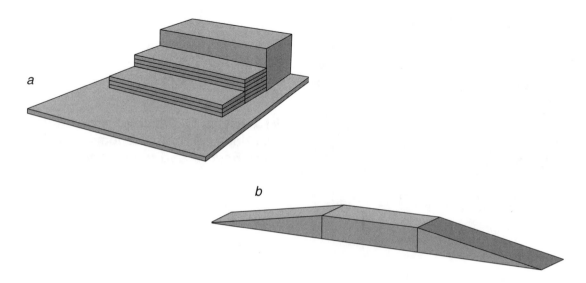

FIGURE 2.5 The stairway *(a)* and the canyon jumper *(b)*.

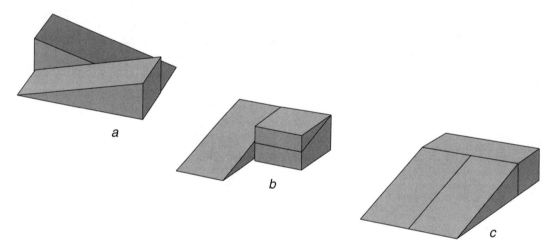

FIGURE 2.6 The escalator *(a)*, the plateau *(b)*, and the big hill *(c)*.

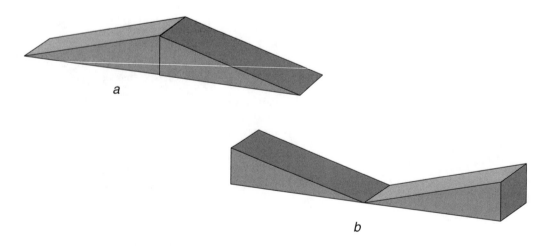

FIGURE 2.7 The mountain peak *(a)* and the valley *(b)*.

a

b

FIGURE 2.8 Pole vaulter *(a)* and low bar with possum pull-up *(b).*

Summary

KiDnastics emphasizes environmental manipulation as an approach to skill development:

- It helps expand movement vocabulary.
- It helps shape specific skills.
- It creates a variety of learning environments.

Creating new and different practice environments is an exciting aspect of teaching KiDnastics. Some of your best ideas will come from new environmental configurations suggested by your students. Be sure to listen to them!

CHAPTER 3

Teaching and Assessing KiDnastics®

Teaching and assessing go hand in hand. A well-designed lesson first will consider the ability and readiness of the learner. Assessment does not have to be viewed as a laborious process of superficial skills testing; it is really an observation that provides teachers with information about students' placement within the learning process to determine where they need to go next. When viewed in this way, assessment becomes an inseparable part of the teaching process. In this chapter we will simplify both teaching and assessment processes in KiDnastics instruction through several examples.

Using the Three-Step Process

Simplicity has been a constant theme in our rethinking of gymnastics instruction. Many years of trial and development have shown us that KiDnastics instruction can be framed around a simple three-step process. These three steps guide teacher functions and student tasks in a progressive way. Figure 3.1 is a brief overview of this three-step process. First the teacher simply needs to choose a skill focus or theme from any of those listed under the five skill categories (rolling, jumping, balancing, vaulting, and hanging and climbing). Next, the teacher proceeds through the three-step process of practicing, then sequencing, and finally performing.

The chart in figure 3.1 provides a simple, brief outline for teachers. Part II of this book provides more detailed examples of step one of the KiDnastics approach. Part III discusses steps two and three.

KiDnastics: Easy As 1, 2, 3!

Get ready! Pick a skill or theme from the five categories

- Rolling (chapter 4)
- Jumping (chapter 5)
- Balancing (chapter 6)
- Vaulting (chapter 7)
- Hanging and climbing (chapter 8)

	Chapter 4	Chapter 5	Chapter 6	Chapter 7	Chapter 8
Suggested target skills and themes	Four basic rolls	Good landings	Static balances	Animal movements	Hanging shapes
	Safety rolls	Five basic jumps	Upright dynamic balances	Wheeling and cartwheeling	Hanging and traveling
	Forward, backward, and shoulder rolls		Inverted balances (tip-ups and head balances)	Front, flank, and straddle vaulting	Rotating
			Inverted balances (hand walks and balances)		Supporting

Step 1: Practicing (chapters 4-8)

- Practice single skills or themes in different environments.
- Practice individually, then with a partner.

Step 2: Sequencing (link skills together to increase complexity) (chapter 9)

- Link skills together *within* and *across* the five movement categories.
- Practice in different environments.
- Practice individually, then with a partner, or in groups.

Step 3: Performing (create, refine, and show work) (chapter 9)

- Create and refine sequences.
- Work individually, then with a partner, or in groups.
- Perform sequence for others.

From *KiDnastics®: A Child-Centered Approach to Teaching Gymnastics* by Eric Malmberg, 2003, Champaign, IL: Human Kinetics.

FIGURE 3.1 Teaching KiDnastics in three easy steps.

Assessment

Because teachers observe students every time they teach, they usually have a sense of their classes' ability levels. But what if someone wanted proof of student learning? Would you be able to provide the proof? Shouldn't you write something down? What kind of measures or scales could you use to assess individual skills and partner sequences? Many teachers have used the following rubrics and other assessment ideas in a variety of settings.

Assessing Individual Skill Competency

The skill assessment in figure 3.2 is adapted from *Children Moving* (Graham et al., 2001) to assess individual skills as well as sequences. Notice how the categories of precontrol, control, utilization, and proficiency can be represented visually by symbols. These symbols can be used as a way to simplify or communicate the scale to children who cannot yet read. Instead of sharing grades, teachers can share the skill assessments.

Assessing Competency in KiDnastics Partner Routines and Sequences

Creating, refining, and performing a KiDnastics sequence with a partner are great ways for students to demonstrate what they know and can do and are excellent examples of authentic tasks. KiDnastics partner performances require students to show proficiency in a variety of skills and provide teachers opportunities to assess several outcomes.

Table 3.1 shows an assessment scale that differentiates among five different skill qualities or outcomes that can be observed within a single KiDnastics partner sequence: flow, amplitude, unison, creativity, and composition.

Assessing Personal and Social Responsibility

The process of creating, refining, and performing a KiDnastics sequence or routine also provides teachers with opportunities to assess affective outcomes, such as responsibility to self and others and safety awareness. To promote these qualities as expectations, some teachers use a full value contract. The full value contract (FVC) is a document that outlines teachers' expectations during a learning experience. The FVC is contractual in the sense that students usually sign it and agree to abide by the provisions of the contract (figure 3.3). An alternative to the written FVC is a spoken oath that all students take in unison that includes the same provisions as those that appear on the written FVC. Another assessment scale (the personal and social responsibility scale) that instructors use to assess personal and social responsibility is shown in figure 3.4.

Assessing Several Learning Outcomes Simultaneously

Students demonstrate several learning outcomes simultaneously in the process of creating, refining, and performing a KiDnastics sequence or routine. A typical KiDnastics routine not only demonstrates student skill achievement but also reveals how well students meet all the instructor's demands, such as construction of the sequence, required elements, creativity, flashy endings, and cooperation.

Question: "What evidence do you have that students are meeting the NASPE Standards?"

Answer: "NASPE Standard 1: A physically educated person . . . shows *competency* in many movement forms and *proficiency* in a few."

Skill Assessment
Adapted from *Children Moving* (Graham et al. 2001)

1 **Precontrol**	2 **Control**	3 **Utilization**	4 **Proficiency**
Looks *awkward*	Repetitions are *more correct*	Replicates with *correctness*	Skill is *automatic*
Each repetition looks different	Repetions are *similar;* student *can replicate*	*Needs concentration* to succeed	Looks *effortless*
Adds extraneous and inefficient *movements* in situations	Skill correctness and *quality decrease when sequenced* or with a partner	Shows control in unpredictable situations	*Refinement* shown *Quality* remains in unplanned situations

 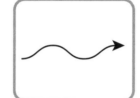 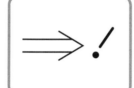 

Assessment item/date

Student's name

1. _____

2. _____

3. _____

4. _____

5. _____

6. _____

From *KiDnastics®: A Child-Centered Approach to Teaching Gymnastics* by Eric Malmberg, 2003, Champaign, IL: Human Kinetics.

FIGURE 3.2 This assessment form is adaptable and can be used for teacher assessment, peer assessment, and self-assessment.

TABLE 3.1 Partner Sequencing Rubric

	Framing	Emerging	Targeting	Exemplary
Flow	Skills performed individually, with constant stops throughout	Skills performed in a choppy fashion, with several hesitations	Rhythmic pattern to skill performance	Deliberate rhythmic changes throughout
Amplitude	Unaware of skill positions and technique	Inconsistent skill positions	Consistent with skill expectations	Extreme range of motion throughout skill performance
Unison	Skills are not done in unison	Waiting, half or fewer skills done in unison	Clearly more than half of skills done in unison	All skills done in unison with precision
Creativity	Movements are duplicating classroom ideas	Shows one new idea or unique combination	Shows more than one unique combination or new connective ideas	Shows unique combinations and new connective ideas throughout the sequence
Composition	Absence of two or more movement categories that could be supported by the environment	Absence of one movement category that could be supported by the environment	Presence of all movement categories that could be supported by the environment	Thorough representation of all movement categories supported by the environment

Full Value Contract

I, _____,
agree to fully honor the following provisions of the following full value
contract:

1. I will demonstrate respectfulness at all times.
2. I will give feedback in a constructive and respectful manner.
3. I will be alert and aware of the safety of myself and others at all times.
4. I will be punctual and attentive at all times.

I am aware that my grade is dependent on my ability to honor the four
provisions of this contract.

5	3	1	0
Exemplary	**Acceptable**	**Needs improvement**	**Unacceptable**
Student **always** honors the four provisions of the contract.	Student **usually** honors the four provisions of the contract.	Student **sometimes** honors the four provisions of the contract.	Student's behavior is **inconsistent** with the four provisions of the contract.

From *KiDnastics®: A Child-Centered Approach to Teaching Gymnastics* by Eric Malmberg, 2003, Champaign, IL: Human Kinetics.

FIGURE 3.3 Sample full value contract.

Personal and Social Responsibility and Safety in Gymnastics

Focus: Safety, diligence, respect for others, self-control

4 = Always demonstrates **care** and **safety** in practice, use of equipment, and spotting.

Always **works diligently** in individual, partner, and small group practice settings.

Always creates a positive experience by **showing respect for others.**

Always maintains **self-control.**

3 = Usually demonstrates **care** and **safety** in practice, use of equipment, and spotting.

Usually **works diligently** in individual, partner, and small group practice settings.

Usually creates a positive experience by **showing respect for others.**

Usually maintains **self-control.**

2 = Sometimes demonstrates **care** and **safety** in practice, use of equipment, and spotting.

Sometimes **works diligently** in individual, partner, and small group practice settings.

Sometimes creates a positive experience by **showing respect for others.**

Sometimes maintains **self-control.**

1 = Seldom demonstrates **care** and **safety** in practice, use of equipment, and spotting.

Seldom **works diligently** in individual, partner, and small group practice settings.

Seldom creates a positive experience by **showing respect for others.**

Seldom maintains **self-control.**

0 = Does not show care and safety, diligence, respect for others, self-control.

Usually needs reminders or prodding from other students or the teacher.

From *KiDnastics®: A Child-Centered Approach to Teaching Gymnastics* by Eric Malmberg, 2003, Champaign, IL: Human Kinetics.

FIGURE 3.4 Personal and social responsibility and safety scale.

Setting: With the gym set up with a variety of KiDnastics environments and children sitting with partners, the teacher explains the task.

Task: "Your task is to **create** and **perform** a partner KiDnastics sequence or routine in any of the stations you see in front of you. You and your partner have _____ amount of time to finish your sequence. After we are finished we will perform our KiDnastics sequence for the rest of the class. Here are some of the things I want you to concentrate on:

1. Try to show good control in all your KiDnastics skills. (skill or sequence quality)
2. Be sure to show a variety of movements such as rolling, jumping, balancing, vaulting, and climbing skills. Don't just do one skill over and over, even if it is your favorite skill. (strategy of required elements)
3. Be sure your routine is at least eight skills long and you finish with a flashy ending. (strategy of required elements)
4. You and your partner need to work well together. This means that you need to work cooperatively and diligently, showing respect for each other; and always work with an eye toward safety." (personal and social responsibility and safety)

Focus: Skill and sequence quality

4 = Shows proficiency of skill; makes sequence appear automatic, smooth, effortless, and refined.

3 = Shows competency of skill; skills or sequences lack some refinement, but they are generally linked smoothly.

2 = Shows control of skills; skill linkage is mostly disjointed or not smoothly connected.

1 = Performs skills with lack of control; skill linkage is disjointed.

Focus: Strategy of required elements

4 = Performs sequence that includes **all** required elements.

3 = Performs sequence that includes **nearly all** required elements.

2 = Performs sequence that includes **some** required elements.

1 = **Cannot** perform sequence with required elements.

Focus: Personal and social responsibility and safety

4 = Always demonstrates **care and safety** in practice, use of equipment, and spotting.

Always **works diligently** in individual, partner, and small group settings.

Always creates a positive experience by **showing respect for others**.

Always **maintains self-control**.

(continued)

From *KiDnastics®: A Child-Centered Approach to Teaching Gymnastics* by Eric Malmberg, 2003, Champaign, IL: Human Kinetics.

FIGURE 3.5 Assessing skill, required elements, personal and social responsibility and safety within a typical KiDnastics task.

(continued)

3 = Usually demonstrates **care and safety** in practice, use of equipment, and spotting.

Usually **works diligently** in individual, partner, and small group settings.

Usually creates a positive experience by **showing respect for others.**

Usually **maintains self-control.**

2 = Sometimes demonstrates **care and safety** in practice, use of equipment, and spotting.

Sometimes **works diligently** in individual, partner, and small group settings.

Sometimes creates a positive experience by **showing respect for others.**

Sometimes **maintains self-control.**

1 = Seldom demonstrates **care and safety** in practice, use of equipment, and spotting.

Seldom **works diligently** in individual, partner, and small group settings.

Seldom creates a positive experience by **showing respect for others.**

Seldom **maintains self-control.**

0 = Does not show care and safety, diligence, respect for others, self-control.

Usually needs reminders or prodding from other students or the teacher.

From *KiDnastics®: A Child-Centered Approach to Teaching Gymnastics* by Eric Malmberg, 2003, Champaign, IL: Human Kinetics.

FIGURE 3.5 *(continued)*

Teachers can tailor each KiDnastics task to meet specific outcomes, and these outcomes can be varied. Figure 3.5 shows a set of rubrics designed to help teachers assess three different outcomes within the same KiDnastics task.

Summary

KiDnastics instruction simplifies gymnastics instruction by following a simple three-step process. Assessment is important to this instructional process; it allows a teacher to keep the learning pulse of the class. In fact, assessment should always drive your teaching. The samples provided in this section should give you a variety of assessment options.

PART II

Practicing Environmentally

STEP 1: Practicing

	Chapter 4	Chapter 5	Chapter 6	Chapter 7	Chapter 8
Suggested target skills and themes	Four basic rolls	Good landings	Static balances	Animal movements	Hanging shapes
	Safety rolls	Five basic jumps	Upright dynamic balances	Wheeling and cartwheeling	Hanging and traveling
	Forward, backward, and shoulder rolls		Inverted balances (tip-ups and head balances)	Front, flank, and straddle vaulting	Rotating
			Inverted balances (hand walks and balances)		Supporting

4

Rolling Environments

Rolling involves rotation. We usually think of rolling around a long (length-wise) or short (crosswise) axis, but rolling can also be asymmetrical (oblique) in its direction and axis, such as in a shoulder roll. All rotation obeys the same efficiency principles, such as roundness, or getting smaller, to speed rotation.

In this chapter we cover the four basic rolls that form the basis of all rolling skills (egg roll, seated roll, log roll, and rocker), then we proceed to the more complex rolls (safety rolls, rolls up and down, shoulder rolls, and forward and backward rolls). Learning to do these rolls in a variety of environments is the focus of this chapter.

The important thing to remember is that competency in one or two rolls on a flat mat does not make a competent roller. Remember . . .

> A good roller can do many
> rolls in many different
> environments!

Rolling Skill or Theme 1
Four Basic Rolls

> ## Let's practice our four basic rolls.

SKILL OR PROGRESSION

Egg roll

Cues for Getting Started

"Make yourself small!"

"Hold your knees tightly!"

"Eggs are crooked rollers."

Performance Points

- Rolling is asymmetrical.
- Rolling does not stop.
- Rolling occurs on all body parts.
- Rolling does not occur in a straight line.

SKILL OR PROGRESSION

Seated roll

Cues for Getting Started

"Rock left and right."

"Feel your weight shift from hand to hand."

"Push to an upside-down push-up."

Performance Points

- **Rotation is around the lengthwise axis.**
- **Body goes from front support to side support to rear support, then returns.**
- **Body stays rigid.**

SKILL OR PROGRESSION

Log roll

Cues for Getting Started

**"Make yourself look like . . .
a long or short pencil!"
a piece of loose spaghetti!"
a long log!"**

Performance Points

- **Body is stretched.**
- **Roll is easier with rigid body but still works with a loose body.**

SKILL OR PROGRESSION

Rocker

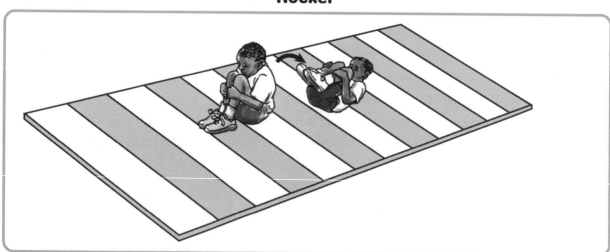

Cues for Getting Started

**"Try to rock back and forth."
"Can you be a rocking horse?"
"Rock big . . . rock small."**

Performance Points

- **Back is round.**
- **Rock is smooth in both directions.**

"Let's change the rolling practice environment!"

Environmental Examples

Log roll *up* the incline

Egg roll *down* the incline

Seated roll with *feet up*

Log roll *across* a panel mat or bench

SKILL STRETCHER

"Pick a card and do that roll in 2 different places."
". . . in 3 different places."

A good roller can do many kinds of rolls in many different environments!

> **Let's try our four basic rolls
> with a partner in unison!**

Partners doing basic rolls in unison on different environments.

Rolling Skill or Theme 2
Safety Rolls

Safety rolling is an important life skill and frequently omitted in gymnastics instruction. Use the following safety roll progressions to help your students become better safety rollers. Competence in safety rolls can prevent or lessen serious injury while students are engaged in activities such as running, landing, jumping, biking, skiing, and so on.

Let's practice our safety rolls.

SKILL OR PROGRESSION
Safety roll from all fours

Cues for Getting Started

"**From a dog stance, melt left, go!**"

"**Now melt right, go!**"

"**Be sure to stay round.**"

Performance Points

- **Body is round.**
- **Many body parts absorb impact.**

SKILL OR PROGRESSION

From a four-point stance

Cues for Getting Started

"From hands and feet touching the floor . . ."

"From a bear walk . . . melt left, go! Now right, go!"

Performance Points

- Body is round.
- Many body parts absorb impact.

SKILL OR PROGRESSION

From a half squat

Cues for Getting Started

"You'll pick up more speed this time, so be sure to absorb the impact with your body and not with your hand."

"From sitting in a chair . . . melt left, go!"

Performance Points

- Absorb impact on arms or side. Do not reach out with hand.

SKILL OR PROGRESSION

From a stand

Cues for Getting Started

"Now from a stand . . ."

"Pretend to wrap your arms around a beach ball to stay round."

Performance Points

- Absorb impact on arms or side. Do not reach out with hand.

SKILL OR PROGRESSION

From a jump

Cues for Getting Started

"Now from a jump . . . land feet first, then safety roll."

"Be sure to absorb the impact with your body and not with your hand."

Performance Points

- Absorb impact on arm or side. Do not reach out with hand.

KiDnastics

Let's change the rolling practice environment!

Easy Entries Into Safety Rolls

Safety roll *down* an incline

Safety roll *across* an incline

Safety roll up onto a panel mat

Try These Entries Next!

Jump from a panel mat, then safety roll

Swing from a rope to a landing mat, then safety roll

A good roller can do many kinds of rolls in many different environments!

" Let's try our safety rolls with a partner in unison! "

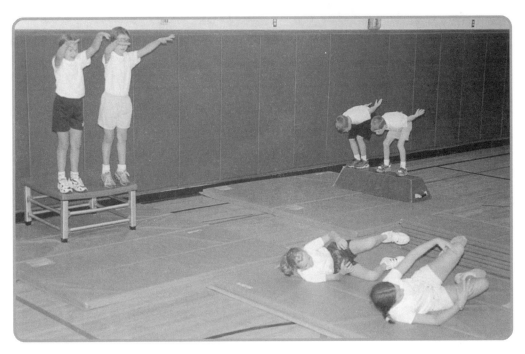

Can you and your partner do safety rolls in all the different environments?

KiDnastics

Rolling Skill or Theme 3
Forward, Backward, and Shoulder Rolls

As a child becomes better at general rolling skills, then he can learn more specific rolling forms. Forward and backward rolls are often taught on traditional flat surfaces. Remember that the flat mat surface is only one environment, and a good roller can negotiate many different environments. An incline mat is the preferred surface on which to explore rolling; however, other environments also help children develop rolling efficiency. Try expanding your students' movement vocabulary with some of these environments and tasks:

> **Let's practice our forward, backward, and shoulder rolls.**

SKILL OR PROGRESSION

Shoulder roll forward (left and right)

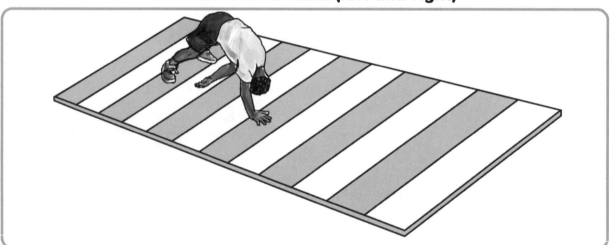

Cues for Getting Started

"Make a bridge, then point and look under." (The child makes a "tunnel" from an all fours position, then looks under and points with one hand backward.)

"Try it left . . . now right!"

Performance Points

- Roll over the shoulder and arm that points under.
- Keep the back rounded.
- Try to stand up at end of skill.

SKILL OR PROGRESSION

Forward roll from a straddle down an incline

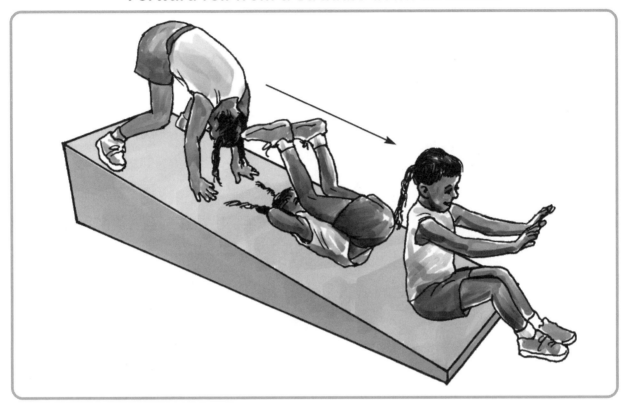

Cues for Getting Started

"Make a big, wide straddle, look under, and go!"

Performance Points

- **Keep the back rounded.**
- **Try to stand up at end of skill.**

SKILL OR PROGRESSION
Shoulder roll backward (left and right)

Cues for Getting Started

"Look over your left shoulder and put your knees there."

"Try it right . . . now left!"

Performance Points

- Keep the back rounded.
- Hands push with flat palms.
- Try to stand up at end of skill.

SKILL OR PROGRESSION

Backward roll down an incline

Cues for Getting Started

"Make moose ears and . . .

keep your chin tucked (bite your shirt)."

rock back and touch your hands to the mat."

Performance Points

- Chin stays tucked.
- Keep the back rounded.
- Hands push with flat palms.
- Try to stand up at end.

"Let's change the rolling practice environment!"

Forward and Shoulder Rolls

Forward and shoulder roll down from knees

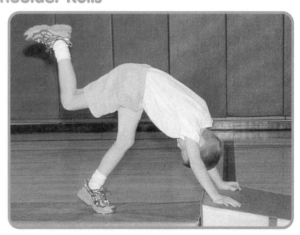

Shoulder or forward roll down an incline from a walk

KiDnastics

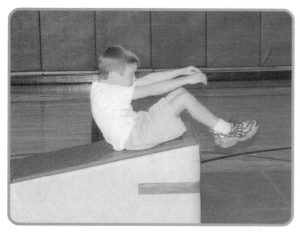

Shoulder or forward roll up an incline to sit on end

Forward roll up onto two stacked panel mats

Forward roll straddled across a jumping box

Roll with a foam ball held between feet, knees, thighs

Backward and Shoulder Rolls

Backward straddle roll on a folded panel mat

Backward roll to a sit on a chair or bench

A good roller can do many
kinds of rolls in many
different environments!

Let's try our forward, backward,
and shoulder rolls with a partner in unison!

Partners practice rolling in unison in different environments.

CHAPTER 5

Jumping Environments

J umping involves the proper use of the legs and the ability to control the body while in the air. In this chapter we suggest several kinds of jumps that children can learn quickly to expand their movement vocabulary. These jumps are presented in a progressive order starting with *good landings* (the S position). Good landings are followed by the five basic jumps. Each of these basic jumps involves a different body shape in the air. Understanding that a good jumper is agile, the teacher can progressively develop this agility through the environmental manipulations shown in this chapter. As learners become better jumpers they can progress from single, controlled jumps to a series of consecutive jumps in different environmental conditions.

Jumping Skill or Theme 1
Good Landings

> **Let's practice our good landings.**

SKILL OR PROGRESSION
The S landing position

Cues for Getting Started

"Make your body like a spring!"

"Make the letter S for safety!"

"Make your spring bounce up and down."

Performance Points

- Knees are bent.
- Arms are in front for balance.
- Body is in S position.
- Eyes focus to front.

Let's change the good landings practice environment!

Expand your students' ability to control their landings by practicing in different environments. Notice how the following environmental conditions slowly increase in difficulty.

Land on a poly spot

Jump and land for distance

Jump to 3 o'clock

Jump *down* to firm surface landing

Jump *down* to soft surface landing

Springboard jump and landing

Jump *up* to a narrow surface landing

Swing, drop, and land

Let's try our good landings with a partner in unison!

Good landings use the whole body, not just the legs!

Jumping Skill or Theme 2
Five Basic Jumps

Let's practice our five basic jumps.

SKILL OR PROGRESSION
Tuck jump (knee slapper)

Cues for Getting Started

"Slap your knees!"

"Make yourself small in the air!"

Performance Points

- Knees are tucked in air.
- Eyes focus in front of landing point.
- Land in S position.

SKILL OR PROGRESSION
Seat kicker

Cues for Getting Started

"Kick your seat with your heels!"

Performance Points

- **Heels kick seat in midair.**
- **Eyes focus in front of landing point.**
- **Land in S position.**

SKILL OR PROGRESSION
Straddle (star) jump

Cues for Getting Started

"Make the letter X!"

"Jump and get wide!"

"Make a big star!"

Performance Points

- **Straddle is wide.**
- **Eyes focus in front of landing point.**
- **Land in S position.**

SKILL OR PROGRESSION

Piked straddle (toe toucher) jump

Cues for Getting Started

"Touch your . . .
  knees.
  ankles.
  toes."

Performance Points

- Straddle is wide.
- Legs are straight, if possible.
- Eyes focus in front of landing point.
- Land in S position.

SKILL OR PROGRESSION
Jump and turn

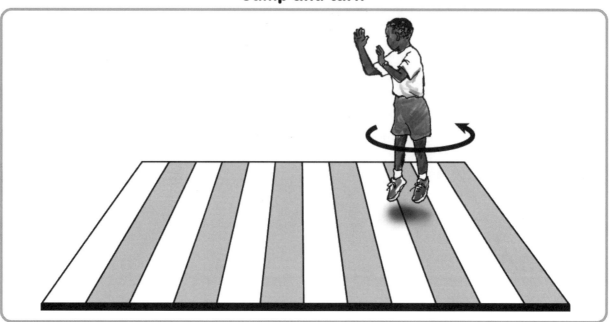

Cues for Getting Started

"Try a quarter turn!"

"Try a half turn!"

"Try a corkscrew!"

"Jump and turn to the east . . . now west!"

Performance Points

- **Eyes focus in front of landing point.**
- **Land in S position.**

"Let's change the five basic jumps practice environment!"

Teachers can extend students' jumping abilities by linking one, two, or three jumps together in a series of jumps that are environmentally different. Create different jump series environments by manipulating some of these environmental variables.

Type of Jump

Tuck jump (knee slapper)

Seat kicker

Straddle (star) jump

Piked straddle (toe toucher) jump

Jump and turn

Other Environmental Variables

1. **Direction of jump**
2. **Number of jumps**
3. **Distance (space) between jumps**
4. **Density or texture of jumping surface**
5. **Height of jumps**

ENVIRONMENTAL EXAMPLES

Zigzag hoops

Tires on a mat

Three, four, or more in a row

Close together

Farther apart

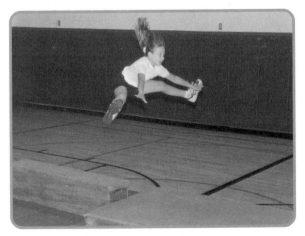

Hard surface to a soft surface

KiDnastics

Height of jump

A good jumper can do many kinds of jumps in many different environments!

" Let's try our five basic jumps with a partner in unison! "

Partners jumping in unison is a challenging extension task.

CHAPTER

6

Balancing Environments

All movements requiring balance—whether static or dynamic, upright or inverted—involve the center of gravity over the base of support. This concept can be illustrated in many ways, such as with pyramid-shaped objects (stable) or inverted pyramid shapes (unstable). Students should understand the principles that determine success in balancing and how some environments can help or hinder their balance when they learn different skills. In this chapter we cover several different types of balances.

Balancing Skill or Theme 1
Static Balances

> ## Let's practice our static balances.

SKILL OR PROGRESSION

N-sit or V-sit

Cues for Getting Started

"Make the letter N with your legs."

"Make the letter V with your body."

Performance Points

- Seat is on floor.
- Hands hold floor for balance.
- Knees are together.
- Toes are pointed.

SKILL OR PROGRESSION

Knee scale

Cues for Getting Started

"All fours! Now stretch one leg back to the wall."

Performance Points

- **Support is on hands, knee, and top of foot.**
- **Leg is stretched backward and upward.**

SKILL OR PROGRESSION

Stork stand

Cues for Getting Started

"Stand still on one leg. Now touch your foot to your knee."

"Try it with eyes open . . . now with eyes closed!"

Performance Points

- **Eyes focus forward.**
- **Body is upright.**
- **Arms are to the side.**
- **One foot is placed on the inside of knee.**

SKILL OR PROGRESSION

Airplane scale

Cues for Getting Started

"Make a T!"

"Make an airplane!"

Performance Points

- Eyes focus forward.
- Foot is at least as high as head.
- Support leg can bend.

SKILL OR PROGRESSION

Y Scale

Cues for Getting Started

"Hold your foot. Now stretch it out to the wall."

"Make a Y!"

Performance Points

- Eyes focus forward.
- Knees are straight.

KiDnastics

“ **Let's change the static balancing
practice environment!** ”

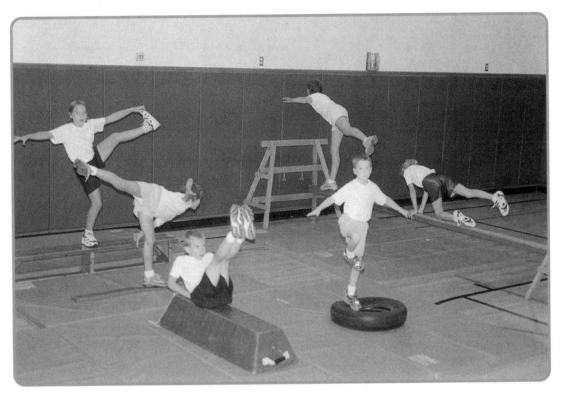

Ask your students to pick a balance card and do that static balance in two, three, four, or more different places.

Skill Stretchers

"Choose a static balance and copy your partner."

"Can you do it with a bean bag on your head or shoulder or foot?"

Bean bags make static balances more difficult.

A good balancer can do many
kinds of balances in many
different environments!

"Let's try our static balances with a partner!"

From left to right: partner triangle, candlestick archway, and double scales.

Upright balances in unison with a partner.

Balancing Skill or Theme 2
Upright Dynamic Balances

Upright dynamic (moving) balance activities need not be limited to the traditional four-inch-wide balance beam. A line on the floor, a rope, a bench, and beams of different widths set at different angles provide a variety of practice environments. If using balance beams or benches, be sure to use appropriate matting and always keep students close to the ground.

 Let's practice our upright dynamic balances.

SKILL OR PROGRESSION
Crawling forward and backward

Cues for Getting Started

"Try a doggie walk!"

"Crawl to the end and touch the end."

"Now crawl backwards."

Performance Points

- Eyes focus in front.
- Hold beam or floor with hands.

SKILL OR PROGRESSION
Forward and backward walking

Cues for Getting Started

"**Tightrope walker.**"

Performance Points

- **Eyes focus at end of surface.**
- **Arms are horizontal and sideways.**

SKILL OR PROGRESSION
Cross over, cross behind

Cues for Getting Started

"**Step over, step behind.**"

"**Grapevine step.**"

Performance Points

- **Eyes focus on footwork and direction of travel.**
- **Arms are horizontal and to the side.**

SKILL OR PROGRESSION

Stand, lie down on the beam (on front, side, or back), and return to stand

Cues for Getting Started

"Take a nap on the beam . . . now wake up and go to school!"

Performance Points

- Move slowly.
- Hold beam or floor with hands.

KiDnastics

SKILL OR PROGRESSION
Jump and switch feet

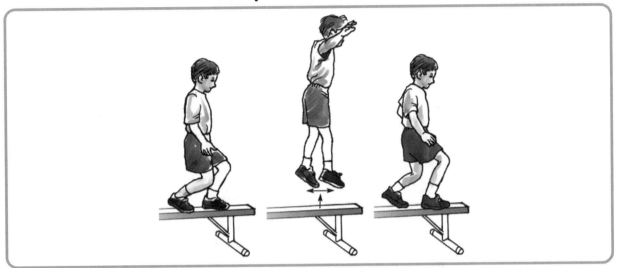

Cues for Getting Started

"Switch and go!"

Performance Points

- Eyes focus on end of beam.
- Arms are horizontal to the side.

SKILL OR PROGRESSION
Hop across beam

Cues for Getting Started

"Dog with a broken leg."

"Hippity hop to the end."

Performance Points

- Eyes focus on end of beam.

SKILL OR PROGRESSION
Pivot turn

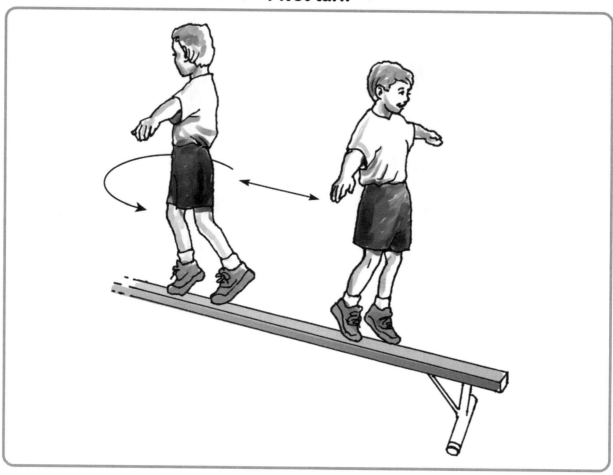

Cues for Getting Started

"Up on your toes and twist!"

Performance Points

- **Posture is upright.**
- **Put left foot in front of right or vice versa.**
- **Rotate on balls of feet.**
- **Eyes focus on beam.**
- **Arms are horizontal and to the side.**

SKILL OR PROGRESSION
Squat turn

Cues for Getting Started

"Stay down low!"

Performance Points

- **Eyes focus on end of beam.**
- **Back stays upright and straight.**

SKILL OR PROGRESSION
Leap

Cues for Getting Started

"Leap over the pop can!"

"Step and stretch."

Performance Points

- Eyes focus on end of beam.
- Land on leg that leads.
- Arms are horizontal and to the side.

SKILL OR PROGRESSION
Backward swing turn

Cues for Getting Started

"Swing your leg backward; now look and turn!"

Performance Points

- Eyes focus on ends of beam.
- Turn is quick.

" Let's change the balancing practice environment! "

Type of Upright Dynamic Balance

Crawling forward and backward	Cross over, cross behind
Forward and backward walking	Pivot turn
Lie down and stand up	Squat turn
Jump and switch feet	Leap
Hop across beam	Backward swing turn

ENVIRONMENTAL EXAMPLES

Balance bench

Standard low beam

Six-inch-wide beam or two-inch-wide beam

A good balancer can do many kinds of balances in many different environments!

> ## Let's try our upright dynamic balances with a partner in unison!

Cross over, cross behind.

Skill Stretchers

"Choose three task cards and link the skills smoothly together with your partner!"

"Now try it in two, three, or four different stations!"

"Can you do it with a bean bag on your head or shoulder or foot?"

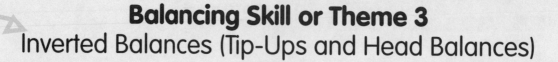

Balancing Skill or Theme 3
Inverted Balances (Tip-Ups and Head Balances)

Inversion, or getting upside down, is a great way to stimulate the inner ear and develop kinesthetic awareness. Rather than focus on the headstand or handstand as a single goal, encourage participation in a variety of inverted tasks by including diverse inverted environments.

> ## Let's practice our inverted balances (tip-ups and head balances).

> ### A good inverted balancer can do inverted balances in many environments!

Special Concerns About Headstands for Special Populations

Overweight children. Overweight and obese children should *not* attempt to put full body weight on their heads.

Down's syndrome. Approximately 10 percent of all people with Down's syndrome have a condition known as *atlantoaxial subluxation*. This condition is an abnormality of the bones and ligaments that maintain the position of the first two vertebrae—the atlas and the axis, respectively. This abnormality permits the spinal column to shift under conditions of physical stress, leading to severe consequences. All Down's syndrome children should have a special X ray to determine whether the atlantoaxial subluxation condition exists before participating in any physical activity. It is the teacher's responsibility to find out the results of this test and act accordingly.

Before beginning hand-supported tasks and skills, be sure to emphasize the proper base of support. Teach and reinforce these four cues:

1. Fingers: Spread apart
2. Hands: Shoulder-width apart
3. Elbows: Straight
4. Eyes: Focusing on fingers

SKILL OR PROGRESSION

Tip-up

Cues for Getting Started

"Sit like a frog!

"Elbows on your knees."

"Weight on your arms."

Performance Points

- **Eyes focus forward.**
- **Fingers are spread apart.**
- **Hands are flat.**
- **Knees are perched on elbows.**

SKILL OR PROGRESSION

Tripod (head balance)

Cues for Getting Started

"Do a tip-up, then lean forward to your head!"

Performance Points

- **Eyes focus on fingers.**
- **Fingers are spread.**
- **Hands are flat.**

Let's change the inverted balancing practice environment!

Tip-Up
Help students find the balance spot in many different environments.

Tripod (Head Balance)
Provide various environments and focus on the task of finding the balance spot instead of doing a perfect head-stand.

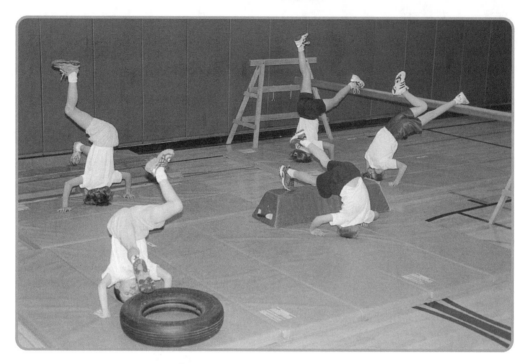

On a raised surface, on a narrow surface, on an inclined surface, using a tire.

Skill Stretchers
"Let's try to find the balance spot in many different environments."

"Now try it tucked, straddled, piked!"

"Can you do it from different starting positions?"

KiDnastics

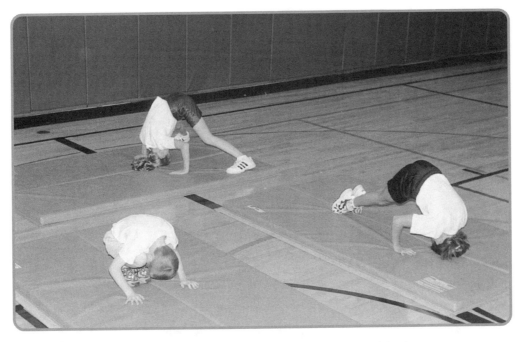

Three different starting positions for trying the head balance.

A good inverted balancer can balance
in many different environments!

 When practicing inverted head balances, be aware of space and location!

"Let's try our tip-up or tripod or head balances with a partner in unison!"

Finding the balance spot with a partner requires good spacing for safety.

Inverted balancing with a partner.

KiDnastics

Balancing Skill or Theme 4
Inverted Balances (Hand Walks and Balances)

⚠️ Before beginning hand-supported tasks and skills, emphasize the proper base of support. Teach and reinforce these four cues:

1. Fingers: Spread apart
2. Hands: Shoulder-width apart
3. Elbows: Straight
4. Eyes: Looking at fingers

> ## Let's practice our inverted balances (hand walks and balances).

SKILL OR PROGRESSION

Switcheroo

Cues for Getting Started

"**Kick and switch your feet!**"

"**Left foot up, now quickly switch right!**"

"**Right foot up, now quickly switch left!**"

Performance Points

- **Fingers are spread apart.**
- **Hands are shoulder-width apart.**
- **Elbows are locked straight.**
- **Eyes focus on fingers.**

SKILL OR PROGRESSION
Hand walks and balances

Cues for Getting Started

"Watch your fingers!"

"Walk left . . .now right!"

Performance Points

- Fingers are spread apart.
- Hands are shoulder-width apart.
- Elbows are locked straight.
- Eyes focus on fingers.

> **Let's change the inverted balancing practice environment!**

Switcheroos (try on surfaces at different heights)

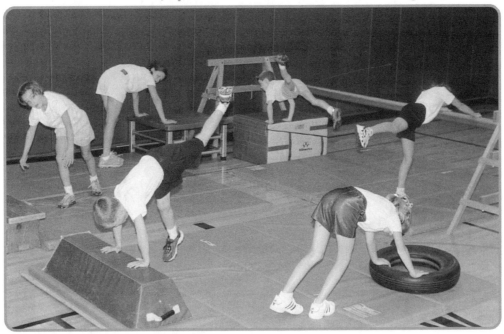

On a mat box, inclined surface, higher surface, narrow surface, and a forearm switcheroo

Hand Walks and Balances

Hand walking up and down

Partner wheelbarrows up, across, down, and around

Shoulder stand

Fall like a tree

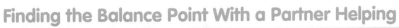

Finding the Balance Point With a Partner Helping

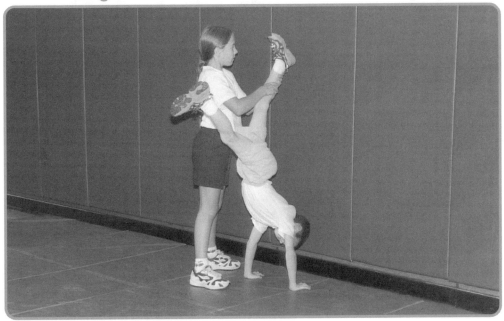

Help lift partner to wall

Help lift partner without the wall

Skill Stretcher

"Can you count to 10 and return?"

A good inverted balancer
can balance in many
different environments!

Let's try our inverted balances with a partner in unison!

Try these hand balancing tasks with a small group.

The log lifter: At least two helpers lift one child and place hands on belly, thighs, shins of the "log." The log keeps eyes focused on hands while lifting to vertical.

Switcheroo circle in unison.

KiDnastics

CHAPTER 7

Vaulting Environments

The word *vaulting* is often associated with traditional gymnastics equipment, such as horses and vaulting boards. The KiDnastics model, however, defines vaulting as moving from one point to another with weight on the hands. This definition describes a movement category, not the equipment or environment used. A good KiDnastics vaulter can move from one point to another with weight on the hands in many different environments.

In this chapter we cover vaulting movements in different environments: animal movements; wheeling and cartwheeling; and front, flank, and straddle vaulting.

Vaulting Skill or Theme 1
Animal Movements

Imitating different animal movements is a good way to get learners to move with weight on the hands.

> ## Let's practice our animal movements.

SKILL OR PROGRESSION

Seal walks

Cues for Getting Started

"Drag your legs behind you!"

"Go forward . . . now backward . . . left."

"Let's hear your seal call!"

Performance Points

- Legs are extended.
- Arms and shoulders are pulling.

SKILL OR PROGRESSION

Bear walks

Cues for Getting Started

"Let's lumber along like a bear!"

"Go forward . . . now backward . . . left."

"Can you growl like a bear?"

Performance Points

- Weight is equal on hands and feet.
- Pace is slow and lumbering.

SKILL OR PROGRESSION

Lame-dog hops

Cues for Getting Started

"Walk like a three-legged dog!"

"Lift one leg and go! Now, faster!"

Performance Points

- Weight is equally distributed on three points.

SKILL OR PROGRESSION
Bunny hops

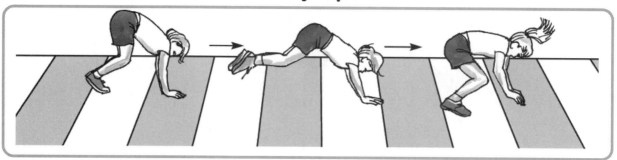

Cues for Getting Started

"Crouch down and spring forward just like a bunny!"

"Let's try two in a row . . . now three!"

Performance Points

- Legs push forward.
- Hands reach forward.
- Weight is on hands first, then on feet.

SKILL OR PROGRESSION
Donkey kicks

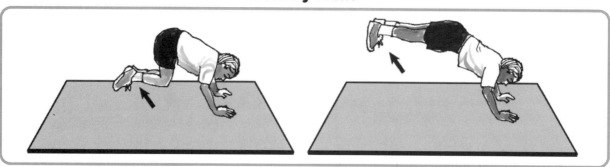

Cues for Getting Started

"Let's kick like a donkey! Knees in, then out . . . now faster!"

"Let's hear you 'hee-haw'!"

Performance Points

- Hands push on floor.
- Knees are tucked to start, then extended to finish.

 Let's change the vaulting practice environment!

Animal Movements

Seal walks

Bear walks

Lame-dog walks

Bunny hops

Donkey kicks

Cues for Getting Started

"Pick a card and do that animal walk . . .

in three different places!"

along a long axis!"

across the short axis!"

ENVIRONMENTAL EXAMPLES

Animal movements in many different environments

Traveling bunny hops

Backward traveling donkey kicks on benches or folded panel mats

Bear straddle travels down a bench

"
Let's try our animal movements with a partner in unison!!
"

The kids are doing lame dog walks, donkey kicks, and seal walks as partner in unison.

Skill Stretchers

"Choose three animal movements and link them smoothly together with your partner. Can your animal walks tell a story? Now try it in two, three, four different places!"

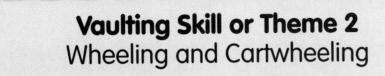

Vaulting Skill or Theme 2
Wheeling and Cartwheeling

Most teachers have few progressions for teaching the cartwheel. Wheeling and cartwheeling are good examples of moving from one point to another with weight on the hands; therefore, they are included in the vaulting movement category.

The following skills explore wheeling as a more general motor pattern and suggest the idea that many different progressions for the cartwheel exist when one first practices wheeling in a variety of environments. The cartwheel, then, simply becomes one type of wheel.

> **Let's practice our wheeling and cartwheeling.**

SKILL OR PROGRESSION

Basic wheel across a mat block or panel mat

Cues for Getting Started

"Hands on and big kick across!"

"Land on the first foot across."

Performance Points

- **Hands are turned sideways.**
- **Hands support weight.**
- **Straddle is wide with feet apart.**
- **Eyes focus on hands throughout.**
- **Landing is on first foot that crosses.**
- **Hands and head face mat at end of wheel.**

Let's change the wheeling practice environment!

Hoop to hoop

Hands *between* parallel bungee ropes and hands over and between a tire

***Up* the incline**

***Down* the incline**

Over the slanted bungee rope
(learner chooses the height)

Around the concentric circles

**Forearm wheeling over two
stacked mats**

A good wheeler can do many
kinds of wheels in many
different environments!

Let's try our wheels with a partner in unison!

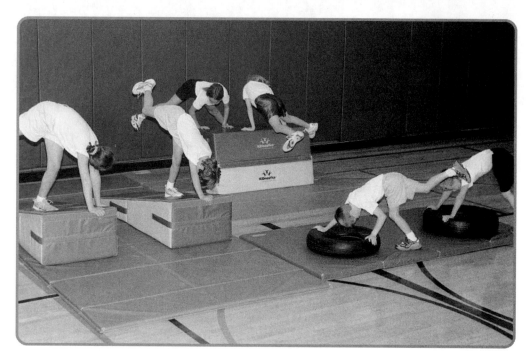

Wheeling with a partner in unison.

Vaulting Skill or Theme 3
Front, Flank, and Straddle Vaulting

The traditional vaults (front, flank, straddle) can be safely taught through modification of the vaulting environment. The following KiDnastics vaulting environments do not employ traditional vaulting horses (which are often hard, narrow, slippery, and too high) but rather a variety of nontraditional surfaces. You will find that these vaulting environments are far easier to work with and virtually eliminate students' fear, injury, and need for spotting.

> ## Let's practice our front, flank, and straddle vaulting.

SKILL OR PROGRESSION

Tucked front vault, stop on top

Cues for Getting Started

"Go slowly . . . stop on top!"

"Squeeze knees and feet together."

Performance Points

- Takeoff is from two feet.
- Stop momentarily on surface top.
- Finish with side toward surface.

SKILL OR PROGRESSION

Tucked front vault

Cues for Getting Started

"Feel weight on your hands!"

"Stay in a tuck; land on your feet!"

Performance Points

- **Takeoff is from two feet.**
- **Motion does not stop.**
- **Body stays tucked.**
- **Finish with side toward surface.**

SKILL OR PROGRESSION

Piked front vault

Cues for Getting Started

"Stay in an upside-down V!"

"Jackknife."

Performance Points

- **Takeoff is from two feet.**
- **Body stays piked.**
- **Land on feet with knees bent.**
- **Finish with side toward surface.**

SKILL OR PROGRESSION

High front vault (round-off)

Cues for Getting Started

"Donkey kick to the ceiling!"

"High wheeler!"

"Feels like a wheel with your feet together!"

Performance Points

- **Takeoff is from two feet.**
- **Body shows extension.**
- **Land on feet with knees bent.**
- **Finish with front toward surface.**

SKILL OR PROGRESSION

Flank vault

Cues for Getting Started

"Two hands to one hand!"

"Stretch sideways!"

Performance Points

- **Takeoff is from two feet.**
- **Body shows extension.**
- **Land on feet with knees bent.**
- **Finish with rear toward surface.**

SKILL OR PROGRESSION
Straddle vault

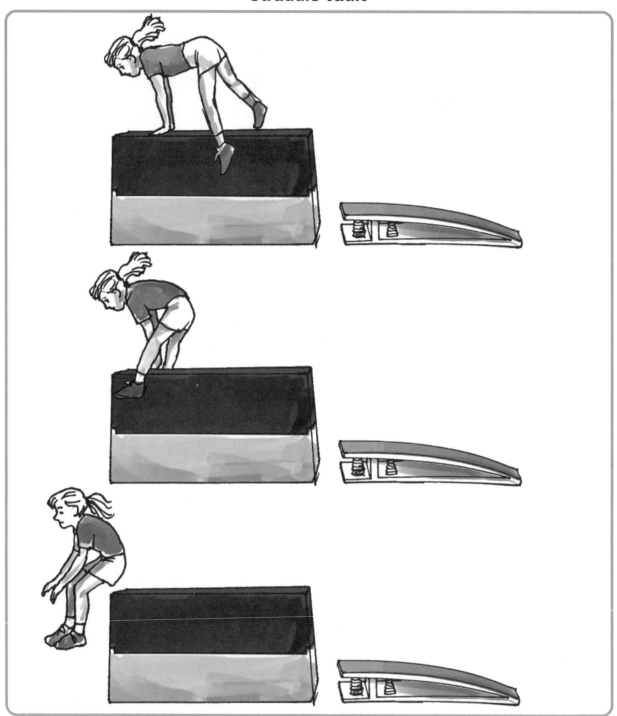

Cues for Getting Started

"Leapfrog it, then sit on the end . . . now all the way over!"

Performance Points

- **Takeoff is from two feet.**
- **Push with hands.**
- **Lands on feet with knees bent.**
- **Finish with rear toward surface.**

KiDnastics

Let's change the vaulting practice environment!

- Vaulting surfaces should not be higher than mid-thigh.
- Use landing mats as a landing surface.

Type of Vault
Tucked front vault

Piked front vault

High front vault

Flank vault

Straddle vault

ENVIRONMENTAL EXAMPLES

Poly dot and foam block without a vault board

Vault board over stacked panel mats

Vault board over foam vaulting box sections

Over a partner

Over foam box sections

 Limit vaulting approach speed by setting the vaulting station a short distance from a wall.

Let's try our vaults with a partner in unison!

CHAPTER 8

Hanging and Climbing Environments

The ability to successfully negotiate hanging and climbing environments begins with the ability to grip with the hands and hang statically. Once learners master the ability to grip and hang, they can progress to the more complex hanging and climbing skills of creating shapes, hanging and traveling, rotating, and supporting the entire body weight. Notice how the first suggested skill or theme in this chapter is static in nature and progresses to more diverse movements involving traveling, then rotating, and finally supporting.

Hanging and Climbing Skill or Theme 1
Hanging Shapes

> **Let's practice our hanging shapes.**

SKILL OR PROGRESSION

Letter N

Letter V

Letter X

Cues for Getting Started

"Hang and make the letter N, W, X, V, or L!"

"Can you do that letter or shape upside down?"

"Can you spell your name while hanging from _____ ?"

Performance Points

- **Grasp with three or four body parts.**

SKILL OR PROGRESSION

Possum pull-ups

Cues for Getting Started

"Can you do six possum pull-ups? Just touch your nose to the bar!"

Performance Points

- **Hold with both hands and feet on top.**

SKILL OR PROGRESSION
Straight inverted hang

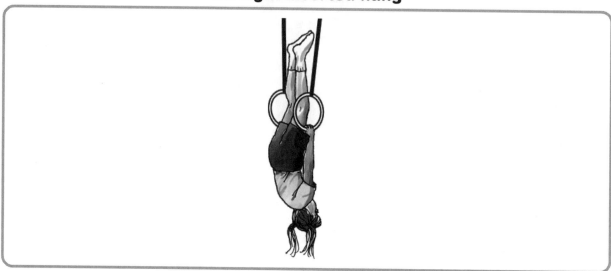

Cues for Getting Started

"Hang straight as a pencil!"

Performance Points

- Eyes focus toward ceiling.
- Knees remain straight.

SKILL OR PROGRESSION
Piked inverted hang

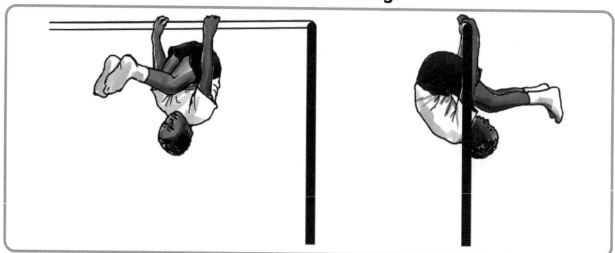

Cues for Getting Started

"Bend in half!"

"Bite your knees!"

Performance Points

- Eyes focus toward ceiling.
- Knees remain straight.

SKILL OR PROGRESSION
Bird's nest

Cues for Getting Started

"Turn inside out!"

Performance Points

- Hold with four body parts.

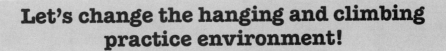

> ## Let's change the hanging and climbing practice environment!

Type of Hanging Shape
Letters and shapes
Possum pull-ups
Straight inverted hangs
Piked inverted hangs
Bird's nest hangs

ENVIRONMENTAL EXAMPLES

Low rings

A rope

Low bar

Higher balancing beam

Parallel bars

A good hanger and climber can hang and climb in many different environments!

Skill Stretchers

"Choose three hanging shapes and try to . . .
do them together with your partner."

"Now try it in two, three, four different places!"

"Can you work together smoothly
to spell your names while hanging?"

"Can you and your partner make these shapes while hanging?"

> " Let's try our hanging shapes
> with a partner in unison! "

From left to right: Piked inverted hang, possum hang, and hanging N.

Hanging and Climbing Skill or Theme 2
Hanging and Traveling

Let's practice our hanging and traveling skills.

SKILL OR PROGRESSION

Possum travels

Cues for Getting Started

"Try possum travels down the tree branch! Now back!"

"Go north . . . now go south!"

"Now try it with just one leg hooked over!"

Performance Points

- Hold with both hands on top.

 Be aware of supports and uprights while traveling.

SKILL OR PROGRESSION

Brachiation (hand over hand)

Cues for Getting Started

"Hand to hand, just like a monkey!"

"Now go backward . . . now sideways!"

Performance Points

- **Hands grip only.**

 Be aware of supports and uprights while traveling.

SKILL OR PROGRESSION

Twists and turns

Cues for Getting Started

"Can you turn a half circle? A full circle?"

"Go north! Now turn around and go south!"

Performance Points

- **Hold with hands or both hands and feet.**

⚠️ Be aware of supports and uprights while traveling.

SKILL OR PROGRESSION
Slanted travel

Cues for Getting Started

"Head first, go uphill! Now feet first!"

"Now try with one foot hooked over!"

Performance Points

- **Hold with hands or both hands and feet.**

 Be aware of supports and uprights while traveling.

SKILL OR PROGRESSION

Pole or rope climb

Cues for Getting Started

"Inchworm up!"

"Squeeze with your feet!"

Performance Points

- Hold with both hands and feet.

 Limit rope and pole climbing to an appropriate height with proper matting.

Let's change the hanging and traveling practice environment!

Types of Travel

Possum travels

Brachiation (hand over hand)

Twists and turns

Slanted travel

Pole or rope climb

KiDnastics

ENVIRONMENTAL EXAMPLES

A rope

Climbing pole

Parallel bars

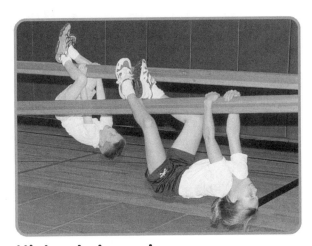

Higher balance beam

⚠ Limit vertical climbing to the ability of the climber.

A good hanging traveler can hang and travel in many different environments!

KiDnastics

> ## Let's try our hanging travels with a partner in unison!

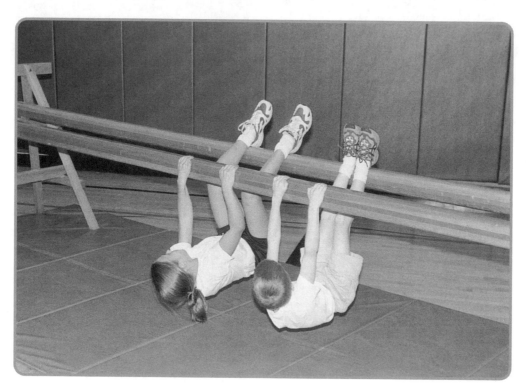

Let kids experiment with their own hanging travels.

Skill Stretcher

"Choose a hanging travel and try to . . .
do it together with your partner."
do it in two, three, four different places!"

Hanging and Climbing Skill or Theme 3
Rotating

Let's practice our rotating skills.

SKILL OR PROGRESSION

Rollover

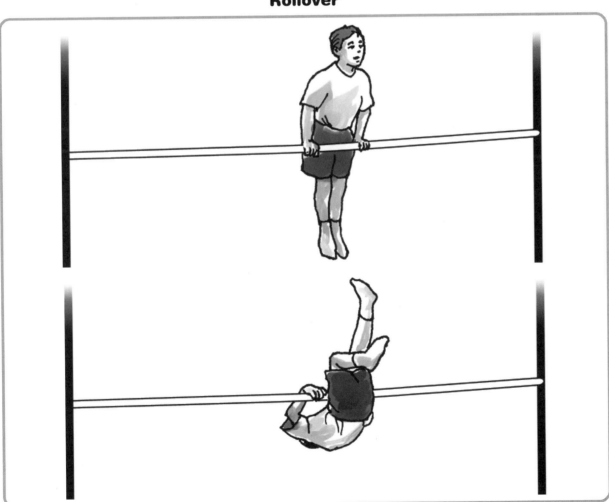

Cues for Getting Started

"Jump up and put your tummy to the bar, then roll it over!"

"Look over, then under and around!"

Performance Points

- Hands grip throughout.
- Body is tucked during rotation.
- Land on feet in S position.

KiDnastics

SKILL OR PROGRESSION
Skin-the-cat over and back

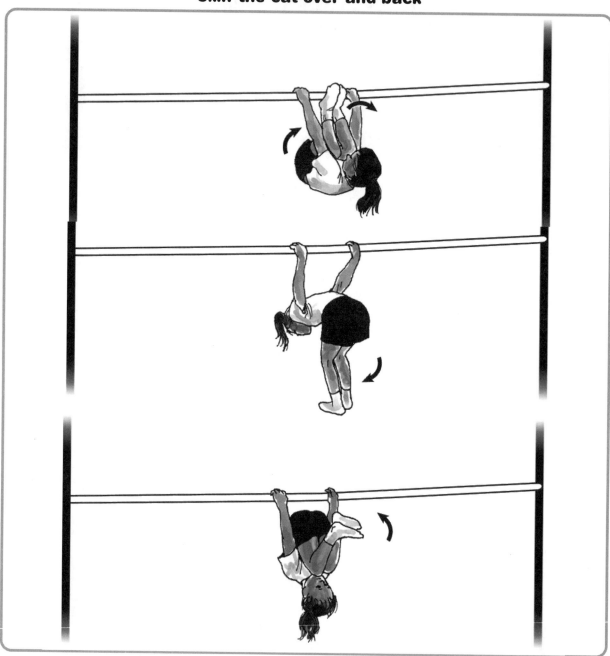

Cues for Getting Started
"Turn inside out!"
"Touch your toes to the floor!"

Performance Points
- Hands grip the bar throughout.
- Feet push off of floor to return.
- Eyes focus on feet throughout.

 Bar should be at chest height or lower. Use adequate matting.

KiDnastics

SKILL OR PROGRESSION
Underswings

Cues for Getting Started

"Swing up and over!"

"Swing under like an S!"

"Lean back, now kick up and go!"

Performance Points

- **Hands release before landing.**
- **Land on feet in S position**

SKILL OR PROGRESSION
Toe-toucher underswings

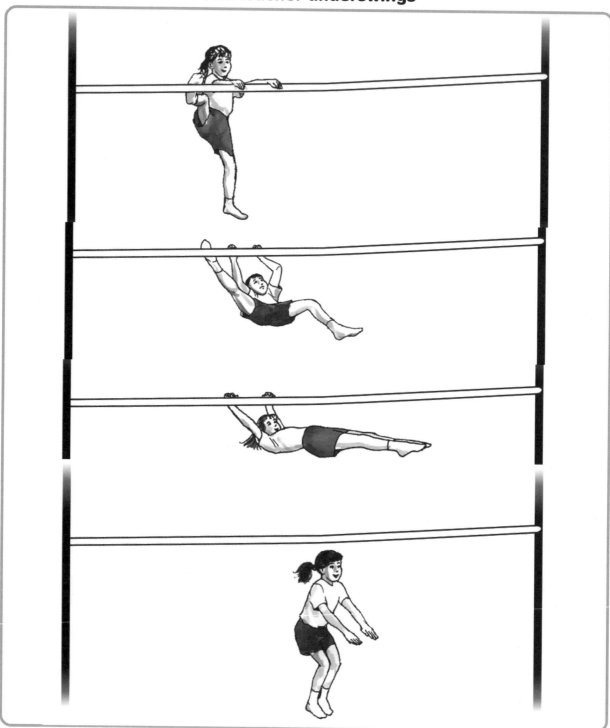

Cues for Getting Started

"Touch your toe . . . now, go!"

"Now touch the other foot . . . now both feet at the same time, go!"

Performance Points

- Hands release before landing.
- Feet stay in contact until under the bar.
- Land on feet in S position.

SKILL OR PROGRESSION
Backward pullover

Cues for Getting Started

"Walk up the ramp, then kick over!"

"Kick the ball over your head!"

"Inchworm up!"

"Squeeze with your feet!"

Performance Points

- Hands grip throughout.
- Chin stays tucked.
- Eyes focus on bar or feet throughout.
- Finish in support.

"Let's practice our rotating skills.

Type of Rotation

Rollover

Skin-the-cat over and back

Underswings

Toe-toucher underswings

Backward pullover

ENVIRONMENTAL EXAMPLES

Over a climber or a balance beam

Low bar and bungee rope

Low rings

Parallel bars

Low bar

Performance Points

- **Adjust low horizontal bars to chest height.**
- **Adjust low rings to chest height.**

Skill Stretcher

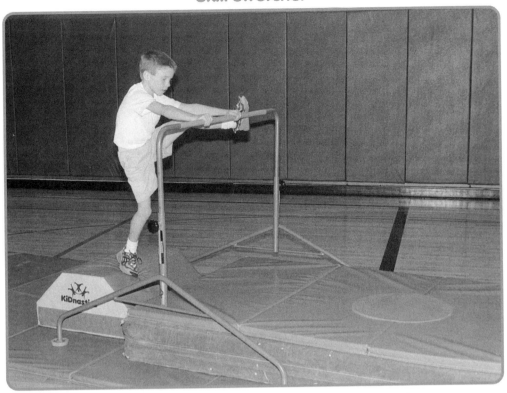

Toe-toucher underswing and landing on a target

> **Let's try our rotation skills with a partner in unison!**

Rotating in unison with a partner requires good communication and timing.

Hanging and Climbing Skill or Theme 4
Supporting

> **Let's practice our supporting skills.**

⚠ Supporting surfaces should not exceed hip height.

SKILL OR PROGRESSION

Hand support

Cues for Getting Started

"Hold on tight and push down hard!"

"Push down, chest up high!"

Performance Points

- Knuckles face forward, thumbs backward (overgrip).
- Posture is erect.

SKILL OR PROGRESSION

Hand support and travel

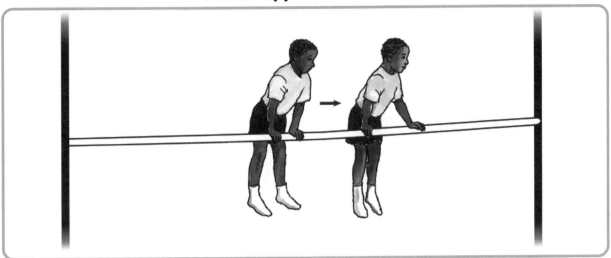

Cues for Getting Started

"Take three hand steps left . . . now, three right!"

Performance Points

- **Knuckles face forward, thumbs backward (overgrip).**
- **Posture is erect.**

SKILL OR PROGRESSION
Hand and leg support

Cues for Getting Started

"Kick one leg over and find the balance point!"

"Try this leg bender and sit!"

Performance Points

- Knuckles face forward, thumbs backward (overgrip).
- Weight rests on leg over the bar.

SKILL OR PROGRESSION

Hip casting

Cues for Getting Started

"Kick your heels backward!"

"Bend . . . then arch out fast!"

Performance Points

- **Knuckles face forward, thumbs backward (overgrip).**
- **Body bends just below beltline.**

KiDnastics

"Let's change the supporting practice environment!"

Type of Support

Hand support

Hand support and travel

Hand and leg support

Hip casting

⚠ Supporting surfaces should not exceed hip height.

ENVIRONMENTAL EXAMPLES

Balance beams as support environment

Low rings

Parallel bars

Beam

Low bar and balance beam

Skill Stretcher
"Try this hip cast and push away to a solid landing!"
"Try to land on different targets!"

Hip cast and push away to a solid landing

KiDnastics

> ## Let's try our supporting skills with a partner in unison!

Supporting in unison with a partner requires good communication and timing.

Sequencing and Performing KiDnastics® Routines

CHAPTER 9

Ideas for Sequencing and Performing

In essence, a KiDnastics sequence involves linking skills together while practicing and performing those skills in nontraditional environments. Students can practice and perform either individually, with partners, or in small groups. An element of creativity is often introduced as students are asked to give their sequence or routine a flashy ending or give a clever name to their work. The teacher is instrumental in designing safe and appropriate environments for students' work. Work on KiDnastics sequences is systematic and progressively develops from simple to complex as students' movement repertoire is expanded.

Sequencing Within the Five KiDnastics Movement Categories

Although there are many ways to develop motor skills progressively, most teachers find it helpful to begin sequencing work by simply linking one skill to another, especially skills that are complimentary in their motor patterns, such as rolls and jumps. Linking one roll to another is a good example of sequencing skills within the same KiDnastics movement category (see figure 9.1).

> **Roll A + roll B = a two-roll sequence**
>
> **Jump A + jump B = a two-jump sequence**
>
> **Balance A + balance B + balance C = a three-balance sequence**
>
> **Hang and climb A + hang and climb B = a two-hang-and-climb sequence**

FIGURE 9.1 Examples of sequencing skills within the same movement category.

Sequencing Across the Five KiDnastics Movement Categories

Another way to link skills together is to combine skills from different categories, or to sequence across the five KiDnastics movement categories. Figures 9.2 and 9.3 show a simple way of doing this.

Teacher-Selected Sequences

Although sequences can be designed across and within movement categories, the actual practice of sequences can occur in a variety of ways. One common way is through predetermined teacher-selected sequences. With this approach, the teacher designs the actual sequence while the students attempt to practice

FIGURE 9.2 Linking skills from two different movement categories: a jump to a safety roll.

Roll A + balance A + roll B = a roll-balance-roll sequence

FIGURE 9.3 Linking skills from three different movement categories (forward shoulder roll to tip-up to forward roll).

and refine the sequence in one or more environments. The instructor makes the decision about what is to be learned; thus, the approach is teacher-centered. Teacher-selected sequences can be useful when the teacher wants to focus on specific skills or sequences or if the teacher has specific skill outcomes in mind. Teacher-selected sequences can also allow the instructor time to assess students' proficiency in certain skill areas.

Task Cards

Task and sequence cards are great vehicles for visually communicating the focus of student practice. The teacher simply provides students with a specific task card that students then interpret and practice.

In the following two sequence card examples (figures 9.4 and 9.5), note how the teacher has made the decision of what to do and in what environment to do it. In the appendix, you'll find single-skill task cards. You can use the possible extension questions and tasks listed in figures 9.4 and 9.5 when working with the single-skill task cards.

Student-Selected Sequences

Another way to design movement sequences and expand movement vocabulary is to allow learners to make choices. Learners simply select skills from a list and link those selected skills together, forming a movement sequence of their own design. Task cards can also be helpful. An easy way to do this is by placing task cards from different movement categories inside hula-hoops. For example, place rolling skills inside a red hoop, jumping skills in a blue hoop, and so on. Students then choose one card from each hoop, thus forming a sequence of movements from the cards drawn (see figure 9.6). Students then begin practicing the sequence in the environments provided.

"Let me see you try this sequence . . ."

Backward roll to a knee scale

Possible extension questions and tasks

- "Can you do this sequence using an incline mat? . . . on the T or H?"
- "Let's do this sequence with a partner in unison!"

FIGURE 9.4 A roll and balance sequence.

"Now let's try this sequence!"

Jump half turn to a backward roll to a knee scale

Possible extension questions and tasks

- "Can you do this sequence in another environment? . . . with two incline mats? . . . on a flat mat? . . . starting with a _____ ? . . . in reverse order?"
- "Let's try this sequence with a partner in unison!"

FIGURE 9.5 A jump, roll, and balance sequence.

"Let's create a roll-jump-balance sequence! Choose one card from each hoop and try that sequence on the environment of your choice."

Hoop 1: Rolling cards

Hoop 2: Jumping cards

Hoop 3: Balancing cards

Possible extension questions and tasks

- "Can you do this sequence in another environment? . . . on the T or H, on the elevator? . . . on a flat mat? . . . starting with a _____?"
- "Can you change the order of the skills? . . . do the sequence in reverse order?"
- "Can you do the sequence with a partner in unison?"

FIGURE 9.6 Students can choose task cards from different hoops to create a sequence.

Performing KiDnastics Work

Showing skills to the rest of the class can be an important conclusion to every KiDnastics lesson. Performing what one has just practiced is a great motivation tool for students and also provides the teacher an opportunity to assess students' growth. The process of practicing and performing is an accountability element and usually helps to keep students on task and focused. In short, practicing should always lead to performing in KiDnastics lessons.

End-of-class performances need not be formal, lengthy, sit-down affairs where one student performs while the rest watch. The following sections describe two quick, informal ways for learners to show their work.

Blast-Off

Students simply perform their individual or partner work at the same time. A simple countdown of "5, 4, 3, 2, 1 . . . blast off!" becomes the signal for all to simultaneously perform. Students can start by performing the switcheroo with partners (figure 9.7), and then the entire class performs the switcheroo at the same time (figure 9.8).

Domino Doubles

With each student standing with a KiDnastics partner, students begin performing in order and in fast succession, like dominoes (see figure 9.9).

FIGURE 9.7 A class performing their partner switcheroos simultaneously on the "blast-off" signal: "All together now! Ready . . . 5, 4, 3, 2, 1, blast off."

FIGURE 9.8 A class in one long line performing the giant switcheroo on the "blast-off" signal.

FIGURE 9.9 Using the domino procedure, teachers can quickly assess large numbers of students. In this example students are performing switcheroos in succession.

KiDnastics Partner Routines: An Authentic Assessment

One of the major aims of KiDnastics work is to help students grow as movers by progressing from singular skills to sequences to longer partner routines of eight or more skills. These longer KiDnastics partner routines serve as a task for students to show what they have learned. Partner routines of eight or more skills allow students to work in a creative and cooperative way to perform an interesting KiDnastics routine of their own design. Figure 9.10 shows a set of guidelines a teacher can follow to help students begin the task of creating KiDnastics partner routines.

The Setting
- Students sit with partners (two or three).
- A variety of nontraditional environments are set up.

Introduction
Teacher explains and identifies the various environments; she ensures that students see that each environment lends itself to different movements they have learned in the five movement categories of rolling, jumping, balancing, vaulting, and hanging and climbing.

(continued)

FIGURE 9.10 A step-by-step approach to helping students create partner routines.

(continued)

Task

1. Develop a creative partner routine that is eight skills long.
2. Skills for progressions must be those that students have already learned.
3. Work in unison with partner(s).
4. Don't forget a flashy ending.
5. Time limit is _____ minutes/classes/weeks.
6. Give your sequence a clever name.

Other ideas

1. Wear coordinated clothing (e.g., matching color, type).
2. Videotape student work for replay.
3. Perform routines to music (for whole class or individual groups).
4. Because all kids can succeed with KiDnastics routines, the activity is an impressive showing at school assemblies and parents' night demonstrations.
5. Give awards for different qualities of work (e.g., hardest workers, best compromisers, flashiest ending, best music, funniest sequence, most synchronized group).

FIGURE 9.10 *(continued)*

Summary

Sequencing and performing KiDnastics routines are important parts of the three-step KiDnastics approach. Students are motivated to excel when they are given the opportunity to showcase their work for the instructor and the rest of the class. The KiDnastics model provides instructors and learners with variety and flexibility in linking together sequences of skills. The choices range from predetermined sequences to student-selected creations. With these choices, students have the opportunity to learn and create various combinations in their lessons, and teachers have the opportunity to observe students' skills in the different environments. Sequencing and performing are easy ways for instructors to move instruction toward authentic performance tasks for assessment.

Organizing and Performing KiDnastics® Shows

Most children who take on artistic or athletic endeavors—whether it be music, gymnastics, dance, or martial arts—do so with the goal of performance in mind. One of the natural outcomes of the three-step KiDnastics approach is the opportunity to create special performance opportunities for individual students and whole classes. A special KiDnastics show or demonstration provides an excellent opportunity for students to display their achievements to others; likewise, it provides an additional opportunity for instructors to evaluate students' performance in a very authentic setting. KiDnastics sequences developed in class can be easily performed at larger events, such as parent groups, or in the form of an open house. Another option can be a presentation linked to a theme, such as a circus, a rodeo, Mardi Gras, outer space, or the Olympics. Organizing these special events involves a bit of foresight and planning. This chapter will help the instructor produce a first-rate KiDnastics show. An organizational checklist is included at the end of the chapter.

What Is a KiDnastics Show?

A KiDnastics show is a special event and usually a more formal demonstration of KiDnastics work than the typical performance work in class. Typically, a

KiDnastics show is a special performance for family members and friends and can involve many participants. Much like a circus, KiDnastics shows are organized into segments to create a program of events.

Why Do a KiDnastics Show?

Although there are many reasons to organize a KiDnastics show, perhaps none is more important than to show parents and guardians exactly what their children have learned. KiDnastics shows also serve these functions:

- Students have opportunities to apply what they know and can do through the creation of a performance.
- A culminating event increases students' motivation and focus.
- A KiDnastics show provides students with an opportunity to be creative.
- A final event gives teachers opportunities to show other aspects of their total program.

Who Can Participate in a KiDnastics Show?

Every kid can perform because the KiDnastics model is adaptable and inclusive to children of all abilities. KiDnastics sequences and routines allow *all* students to show what they *can* do in environments of *their choice*. As a rule, children gravitate toward environments that promote personal movement, so even children with disabilities can create KiDnastics sequences. Teachers must be involved with adapting the environments to each student's specific disability. The adaptation of environments to aid students with disabilities is one of the most rewarding attributes of the KiDnastics model.

Invitations to a KiDnastics Show

Lack of parent attendance at school or student functions can be a frustrating issue for teachers. One way to increase involvement is through a personal invitation from the child to the parent or guardian (see figure 10.1).

Newsletters

No matter what type of setting you are teaching a KiDnastics program—whether it be a recreation program, sport school, physical education, or sports camp—keeping parents and guardians informed about what is happening in your classes is an important part of a successful program. Newsletters are a great way to keep all informed.

Some instructors spend much time creating newsletters that are elaborate and graphically appealing, whereas others simply send home one-page handwritten

You Are Invited to a Gymnastics Jamboree!

Come support your son or daughter as they take part in the Fifth Annual KiDnastics® Talent Show. Your child has worked very hard in mastering the many great skills that KiDnastics has to offer. Each group will perform their own devised sequence to be judged by you, the parents. Each group will be given their own rewards and prizes. Everyone leaves a winner at Sylvan Avenue Elementary.

Place: Sylvan Avenue Elementary School

Date: February 25

Time: 7:00 p.m.

For further information or questions regarding the event, please feel free to contact our main office at 555-3800.

We are looking forward to seeing you there!

Top Five Reasons to Come Watch Me

5. I am an educated mover.
4. I work well with others.
3. I enjoy KiDnastics.
2. See where your money goes.
1. You love me.

FIGURE 10.1   **Sample invitation to a KiDnastics culminating event.**

notes. See figure 10.2 for guidelines for writing a newsletter. Regardless of which approach you adopt, a good newsletter need only address two questions:

1. What have we been *doing* and *learning* while in class?
2. What questions should I (the parent or guardian) ask my son or daughter?

Summary

KiDnastics shows are exciting and memorable culminating events for students. With the organization and communication tools suggested in this chapter, the teacher can better ensure a well-organized event. Teachers can use the checklist in figure 10.3 to guide them in organizing a KiDnastics event.

Hillsdale _____ School
Physical Education Newsletter

Dear Parents:

Introduce a gymnastics unit coming up in the next two weeks.

Explain the benefits of developing gymnastics-type skills, and relate it to the idea of a physically educated person.

Give a *brief* idea of what the parents should expect the student to be able to *know* (cognitive) and *do* (psychomotor) by the end of the unit.

Emphasize that safety is important, and make parents aware of some of the rules and behavioral expectations.

Ask whether their child has any specific medical conditions or limitations you (the teacher) should be aware of.

Invite the parents to class for a visit.

Thank them.

Yours in education,

The Hillsdale _____ School Physical Education Staff

Mr., Ms., Mrs. _____

Mr., Ms., Mrs. _____

Mr., Ms., Mrs. _____

Hillsdale _____ School
"Creating Physically Educated Children"

FIGURE 10.2 Guidelines for writing a newsletter.

KiDnastics® Show Checklist

_____ Set date and time for performance (midweek, evening, lunchtime).

_____ Optional: Do you want to emphasize a theme (rodeo, circus, outer space)?

_____ Be sure all individuals, groups, classes have ample practice time before the show date.

_____ Will there be a dress rehearsal? When?

_____ Identify KiDnastics environments or other equipment needed for each group or class.

Parent invitation or newsletter

_____ Design parent invitation or newsletter.

_____ Run copies.

_____ Send invitation or newsletter home 10 days before show.

_____ Send brief reminder home three days before show.

Music

_____ Will all groups select their own music?

_____ Will the teacher select the music?

_____ Screen music for appropriateness (tempo, volume, lyrics).

Program (schedule of events)

_____ Organize the schedule of events for the show (determine content and order).

_____ Design program contents, cover page, and artwork. Be sure to include all kids' names.

Performer concerns

_____ Be sure students understand their tasks and rules during the show.

_____ Performers (all kids).

_____ Equipment movers (some kids).

_____ Announcer or narrator (one or two kids).

_____ Create a script for announcer or narrator.

Be sure students have created sequences that have the following elements

_____ Match the theme (optional) you have established

_____ A definite beginning

_____ A flashy ending

_____ A clever group name

_____ Coordinated clothing or costumes

FIGURE 10.3 Use this checklist to organize your own **KiDnastics show.**

From _KiDnastics: A Child-Centered Approach to Teaching Gymnastics_ by Eric Malmberg, 2003, Champaign, IL: Human Kinetics.

Conclusion

KiDnastics emerged out of innocent curiosity and the need to rethink gymnastics instruction in ways that made sense. This book is an effort to help teachers; however, it was children who provided the answers. Simplicity is at the core of KiDnastics teaching, and we believe that nothing sums it up better than the following schematic:

Get Ready: Pick a Skill or Theme
- Rolling
- Jumping
- Balancing
- Vaulting
- Hanging and climbing

Step 1: Practicing
- Practice single skills or themes in different environments.
- Practice individually, then with a partner.

Step 2: Sequencing
- Link skills together *within* and *across* the five movement categories.
- Practice in different environments.
- Practice individually, then with partners, in groups of three, four, and so on.

Step 3: Performing
- Creating, refining, then showing work.
- Work alone or with partners, in groups of three, four, and so on.

We were excited to recently learn that teachers in some other countries have also begun to create new and different ways of teaching gymnastics. My colleague Wolfgang Krause, at the Deutsches Sporthochschule in Cologne, explained that today there is a virtual renaissance in gymnastics thinking going on in Germany. As a result new forms of gymnastics have emerged there, such as cooperative gymnastics (Gerling, 1997) and adventure gymnastics. The development of these new models grew out of asking some good questions like:

- What is gymnastics?
- What aims or objectives do I have when I teach gymnastics?

Nearing his retirement Hayes Kruger, of movement education fame, suggested that we need to drop the word *gymnastics* and replace it with the term *body management* because that was usually the functional aim of gymnastics teaching. We believe that KiDnastics is not only a name change but also an important attempt to rethink gymnastics teaching in its entirety. If good ideas are born of good questions, why did it take us so long to ask children, "What kind of gymnastics would *you* invent?" KiDnastics was their answer.

Bibliography

Chepko, S., & Arnold, R.K. (eds.). (2000). *Guidelines for physical education programs, grades K-12.* Needham Heights, MA: Allyn & Bacon.

Diem, L. (1960). *Who can . . . ,* 2nd edition. Frankfurt, Germany: Wilhelm Limpert.

Fodero, J., & Furblur, E. (1989). *Creating gymnastic pyramids and balances.* Champaign, IL: Leisure Press/Human Kinetics.

Gerling, I. (1997). *Teaching children's gymnastics.* Stolberg, Germany: Verlag & Druck.

Graham, G., Holt-Hale, S., & Parker, M. (2001). *Children moving: A reflective approach to teaching physical education,* 5th edition. Mountain View, CA: Mayfield.

Hacker, P., Malmberg, E., Nance, J., Tilove, A., & True, S. (1992). *Sequential gymnastics II: The instructor's guide,* 3rd edition. Indianapolis: USA Gymnastics.

Hacker, P., Malmberg, E., & Nance, J. (1996). *Gymnastics fun and games.* Champaign, IL: Human Kinetics.

O'Quinn, G. (1990). *Teaching developmental gymnastics: Skills to take through life.* Austin, TX: University of Texas Press.

Rink, J. (1993). *Teaching physical education for learning.* St. Louis: Mosby-Yearbook.

Rink, J., Dotson, C., Franck, M., Hensley, L., Holt-Hale, S., Lund, J., Payne, G., & Wood, T. (eds.). (1995). *Moving into the future: National standards for physical education.* Reston, VA: AAHPERD/NASPE.

Schembri, G. (1990). *Aussie gym fun: A resource for schools and clubs.* Melbourne: Australian Gymnastics Federation.

United States Gymnastics Federation. (1992). *I can do gymnastics: Essential skills for beginning gymnasts.* Indianapolis: Masters Press.

Werner, P. (1994). *Teaching children gymnastics.* Champaign, IL: Human Kinetics.

Whitlock, S. (ed.). (1998). *USA Gymnastics Safety Handbook for Gymnastics and Other Sport Activities,* January, 1998 edition. Indianapolis: USA Gymnastics.

Task Cards

Egg Roll

From *KIDnastics®: A Child-Centered Approach to Teaching Gymnastics* by Eric Malmberg, 2003, Champaign, IL: Human Kinetics.

Seated Roll

From *KIDnastics®: A Child-Centered Approach to Teaching Gymnastics* by Eric Malmberg, 2003, Champaign, IL: Human Kinetics.

Log Roll

From *KIDnastics®: A Child-Centered Approach to Teaching Gymnastics* by Eric Malmberg, 2003, Champaign, IL: Human Kinetics.

Rocker

From *KIDnastics®: A Child-Centered Approach to Teaching Gymnastics* by Eric Malmberg, 2003, Champaign, IL: Human Kinetics.

Safety Roll From all Fours

From *KiDnastics®: A Child-Centered Approach to Teaching Gymnastics* by Eric Malmberg, 2003, Champaign, IL: Human Kinetics.

Safety Roll From a Four-Point Stance

From *KiDnastics®: A Child-Centered Approach to Teaching Gymnastics* by Eric Malmberg, 2003, Champaign, IL: Human Kinetics.

Safety Roll From a Half Squat

From *KiDnastics®: A Child-Centered Approach to Teaching Gymnastics* by Eric Malmberg, 2003, Champaign, IL: Human Kinetics.

Safety Roll From a Stand

From *KiDnastics®: A Child-Centered Approach to Teaching Gymnastics* by Eric Malmberg, 2003, Champaign, IL: Human Kinetics.

Safety Roll
From a Jump

From *KiDnastics®: A Child-Centered Approach to Teaching Gymnastics* by Eric Malmberg, 2003, Champaign, IL: Human Kinetics.

Shoulder Roll
Forward
(Left and Right)

From *KiDnastics®: A Child-Centered Approach to Teaching Gymnastics* by Eric Malmberg, 2003, Champaign, IL: Human Kinetics.

Forward Roll
From a Straddle
Down an Incline

From *KiDnastics®: A Child-Centered Approach to Teaching Gymnastics* by Eric Malmberg, 2003, Champaign, IL: Human Kinetics.

Shoulder Roll
Backward
(Left and Right)

From *KiDnastics®: A Child-Centered Approach to Teaching Gymnastics* by Eric Malmberg, 2003, Champaign, IL: Human Kinetics.

Backward Roll
Down an Incline

From *KiDnastics®: A Child-Centered Approach to Teaching Gymnastics* by Eric Malmberg. 2003, Champaign, IL: Human Kinetics.

From *KiDnastics®: A Child-Centered Approach to Teaching Gymnastics* by Eric Malmberg. 2003, Champaign, IL: Human Kinetics.

From *KiDnastics®: A Child-Centered Approach to Teaching Gymnastics* by Eric Malmberg. 2003, Champaign, IL: Human Kinetics.

From *KiDnastics®: A Child-Centered Approach to Teaching Gymnastics* by Eric Malmberg. 2003, Champaign, IL: Human Kinetics.

The S Landing Position

From *KiDnastics®: A Child-Centered Approach to Teaching Gymnastics* by Eric Malmberg. 2003, Champaign, IL: Human Kinetics.

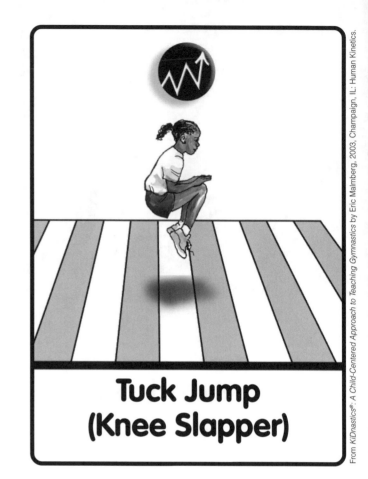

Tuck Jump (Knee Slapper)

From *KiDnastics®: A Child-Centered Approach to Teaching Gymnastics* by Eric Malmberg. 2003, Champaign, IL: Human Kinetics.

Seat Kicker

From *KiDnastics®: A Child-Centered Approach to Teaching Gymnastics* by Eric Malmberg. 2003, Champaign, IL: Human Kinetics.

Straddle (Star) Jump

From *KiDnastics®: A Child-Centered Approach to Teaching Gymnastics* by Eric Malmberg. 2003, Champaign, IL: Human Kinetics.

Piked Straddle (Toe Toucher) Jump

From *KiDnastics®: A Child-Centered Approach to Teaching Gymnastics* by Eric Malmberg. 2003, Champaign, IL: Human Kinetics.

Jump and Turn

From *KiDnastics®: A Child-Centered Approach to Teaching Gymnastics* by Eric Malmberg. 2003, Champaign, IL: Human Kinetics.

From *KiDnastics®: A Child-Centered Approach to Teaching Gymnastics* by Eric Malmberg. 2003, Champaign, IL: Human Kinetics.

From *KiDnastics®: A Child-Centered Approach to Teaching Gymnastics* by Eric Malmberg. 2003, Champaign, IL: Human Kinetics.

N-Sit or V-Sit

From *KIDnastics®: A Child-Centered Approach to Teaching Gymnastics* by Eric Malmberg, 2003, Champaign, IL: Human Kinetics.

Knee Scale

From *KIDnastics®: A Child-Centered Approach to Teaching Gymnastics* by Eric Malmberg, 2003, Champaign, IL: Human Kinetics.

Stork Stand

From *KIDnastics®: A Child-Centered Approach to Teaching Gymnastics* by Eric Malmberg, 2003, Champaign, IL: Human Kinetics.

Airplane Scale

From *KIDnastics®: A Child-Centered Approach to Teaching Gymnastics* by Eric Malmberg, 2003, Champaign, IL: Human Kinetics.

Y Scale

From *KiDnastics®: A Child-Centered Approach to Teaching Gymnastics* by Eric Malmberg, 2003, Champaign, IL: Human Kinetics.

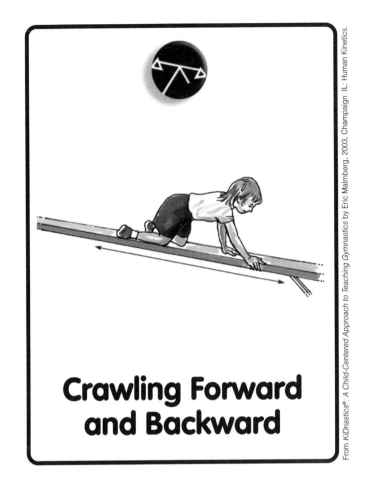

Crawling Forward and Backward

From *KiDnastics®: A Child-Centered Approach to Teaching Gymnastics* by Eric Malmberg, 2003, Champaign, IL: Human Kinetics.

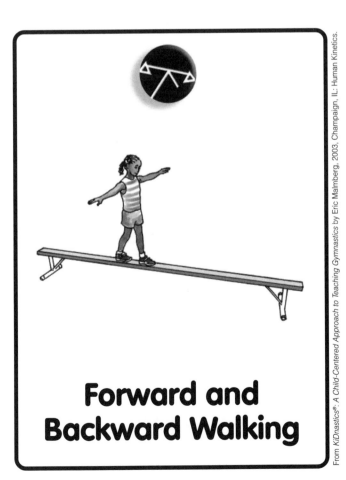

Forward and Backward Walking

From *KiDnastics®: A Child-Centered Approach to Teaching Gymnastics* by Eric Malmberg, 2003, Champaign, IL: Human Kinetics.

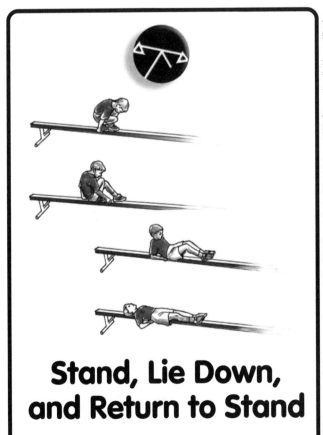

Stand, Lie Down, and Return to Stand

From *KiDnastics®: A Child-Centered Approach to Teaching Gymnastics* by Eric Malmberg, 2003, Champaign, IL: Human Kinetics.

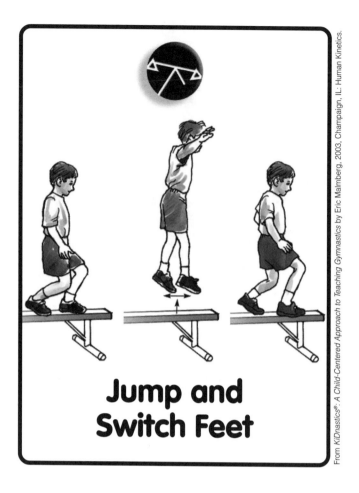

Jump and Switch Feet

From *KiDnastics®: A Child-Centered Approach to Teaching Gymnastics* by Eric Malmberg, 2003, Champaign, IL: Human Kinetics.

Hop Across Beam

From *KiDnastics®: A Child-Centered Approach to Teaching Gymnastics* by Eric Malmberg, 2003, Champaign, IL: Human Kinetics.

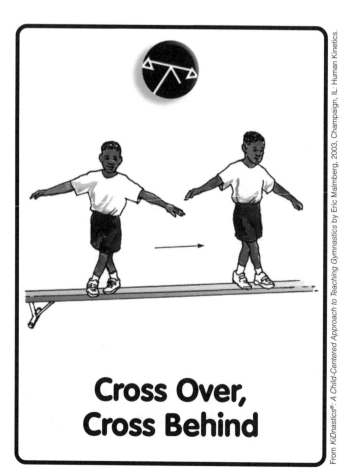

Cross Over, Cross Behind

From *KiDnastics®: A Child-Centered Approach to Teaching Gymnastics* by Eric Malmberg, 2003, Champaign, IL: Human Kinetics.

Pivot Turn

From *KiDnastics®: A Child-Centered Approach to Teaching Gymnastics* by Eric Malmberg, 2003, Champaign, IL: Human Kinetics.

Squat Turn

From *KiDnastics®: A Child-Centered Approach to Teaching Gymnastics* by Eric Malmberg, 2003, Champaign, IL: Human Kinetics.

Leap

From *KiDnastics®: A Child-Centered Approach to Teaching Gymnastics* by Eric Malmberg, 2003, Champaign, IL: Human Kinetics.

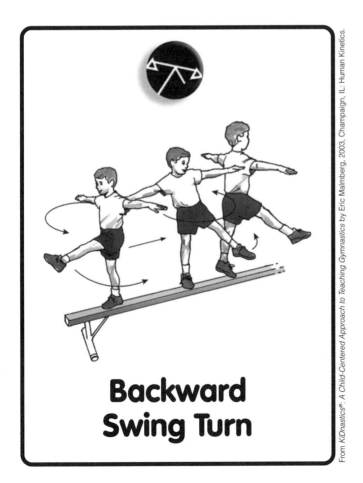

Backward Swing Turn

From *KiDnastics®: A Child-Centered Approach to Teaching Gymnastics* by Eric Malmberg, 2003, Champaign, IL: Human Kinetics.

Tip-Up

From *KiDnastics®: A Child-Centered Approach to Teaching Gymnastics* by Eric Malmberg, 2003, Champaign, IL: Human Kinetics.

Tripod
(Head Balance)

From *KiDnastics®: A Child-Centered Approach to Teaching Gymnastics* by Eric Malmberg, 2003, Champaign, IL: Human Kinetics.

Switcheroo

From *KiDnastics®: A Child-Centered Approach to Teaching Gymnastics* by Eric Malmberg, 2003, Champaign, IL: Human Kinetics.

Hand Walks
and Balances

From *KiDnastics®: A Child-Centered Approach to Teaching Gymnastics* by Eric Malmberg, 2003, Champaign, IL: Human Kinetics.

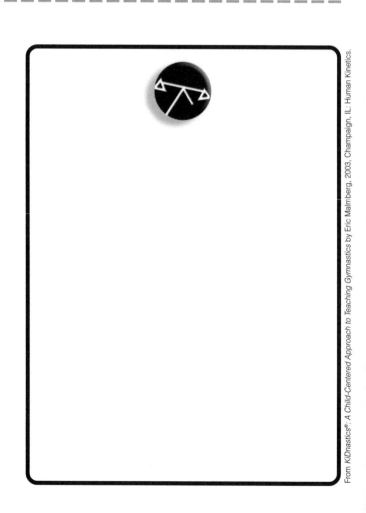

From *KiDnastics®: A Child-Centered Approach to Teaching Gymnastics* by Eric Malmberg, 2003, Champaign, IL: Human Kinetics.

Seal Walks

From *KIDnastics®: A Child-Centered Approach to Teaching Gymnastics* by Eric Malmberg, 2003, Champaign, IL: Human Kinetics.

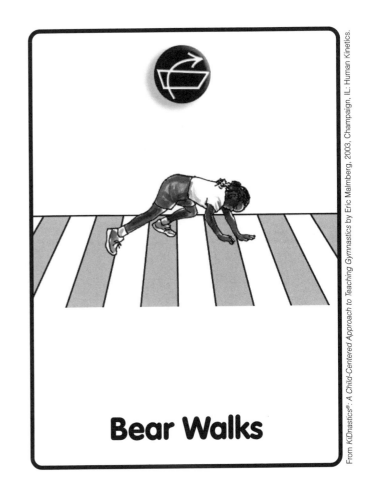

Bear Walks

From *KIDnastics®: A Child-Centered Approach to Teaching Gymnastics* by Eric Malmberg, 2003, Champaign, IL: Human Kinetics.

Lame-Dog Hops

From *KIDnastics®: A Child-Centered Approach to Teaching Gymnastics* by Eric Malmberg, 2003, Champaign, IL: Human Kinetics.

Bunny Hops

From *KIDnastics®: A Child-Centered Approach to Teaching Gymnastics* by Eric Malmberg, 2003, Champaign, IL: Human Kinetics.

Donkey Kicks

From *KiDnastics®: A Child-Centered Approach to Teaching Gymnastics* by Eric Malmberg, 2003, Champaign, IL: Human Kinetics.

Basic Wheel Across a Mat Block

From *KiDnastics®: A Child-Centered Approach to Teaching Gymnastics* by Eric Malmberg, 2003, Champaign, IL: Human Kinetics.

Tucked Front Vault, Stop on Top

From *KiDnastics®: A Child-Centered Approach to Teaching Gymnastics* by Eric Malmberg, 2003, Champaign, IL: Human Kinetics.

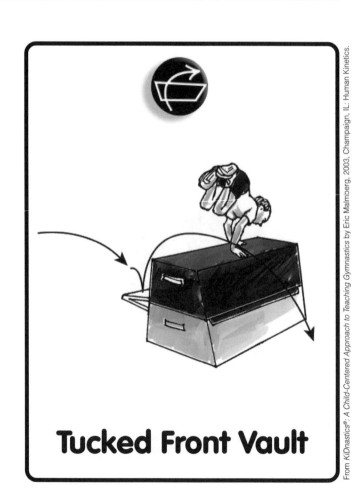

Tucked Front Vault

From *KiDnastics®: A Child-Centered Approach to Teaching Gymnastics* by Eric Malmberg, 2003, Champaign, IL: Human Kinetics.

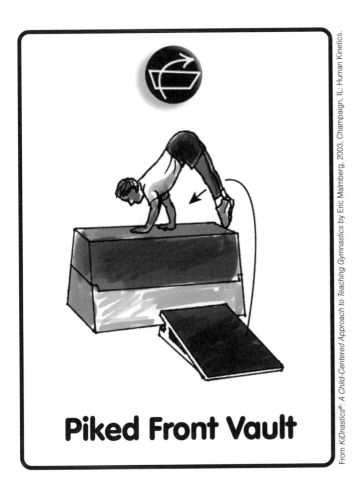

Piked Front Vault

From *KiDnastics®: A Child-Centered Approach to Teaching Gymnastics* by Eric Malmberg, 2003, Champaign, IL: Human Kinetics.

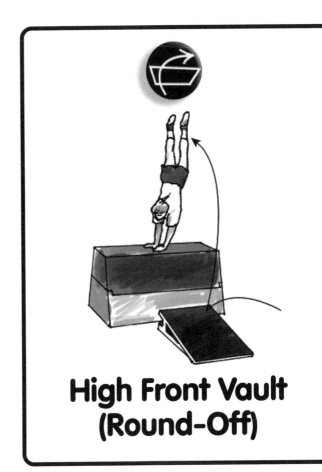

High Front Vault (Round-Off)

From *KiDnastics®: A Child-Centered Approach to Teaching Gymnastics* by Eric Malmberg, 2003, Champaign, IL: Human Kinetics.

Flank Vault

From *KiDnastics®: A Child-Centered Approach to Teaching Gymnastics* by Eric Malmberg, 2003, Champaign, IL: Human Kinetics.

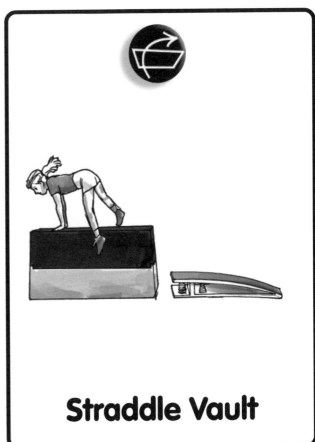

Straddle Vault

From *KiDnastics®: A Child-Centered Approach to Teaching Gymnastics* by Eric Malmberg, 2003, Champaign, IL: Human Kinetics.

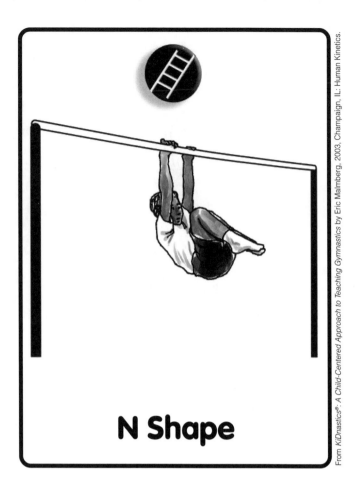

N Shape

From *KiDnastics®: A Child-Centered Approach to Teaching Gymnastics* by Eric Malmberg, 2003, Champaign, IL: Human Kinetics.

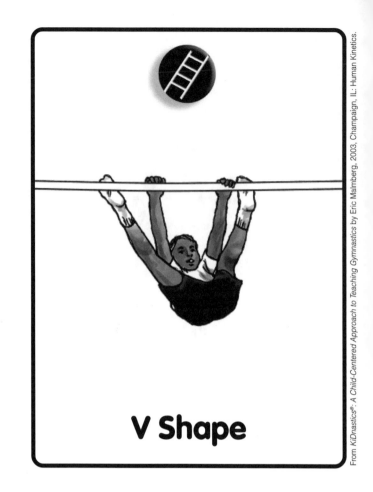

V Shape

From *KiDnastics®: A Child-Centered Approach to Teaching Gymnastics* by Eric Malmberg, 2003, Champaign, IL: Human Kinetics.

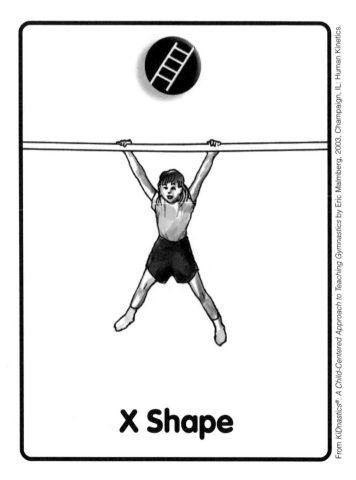

X Shape

From *KiDnastics®: A Child-Centered Approach to Teaching Gymnastics* by Eric Malmberg, 2003, Champaign, IL: Human Kinetics.

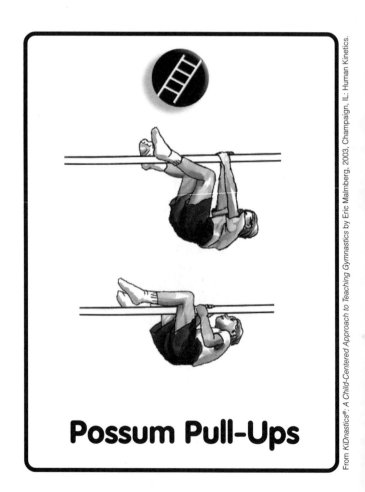

Possum Pull-Ups

From *KiDnastics®: A Child-Centered Approach to Teaching Gymnastics* by Eric Malmberg, 2003, Champaign, IL: Human Kinetics.

Straight
Inverted Hang

From *KiDnastics®: A Child-Centered Approach to Teaching Gymnastics* by Eric Malmberg, 2003, Champaign, IL: Human Kinetics.

Piked Inverted Hang

From *KiDnastics®: A Child-Centered Approach to Teaching Gymnastics* by Eric Malmberg, 2003, Champaign, IL: Human Kinetics.

Bird's Nest

From *KiDnastics®: A Child-Centered Approach to Teaching Gymnastics* by Eric Malmberg, 2003, Champaign, IL: Human Kinetics.

Possum Travels

From *KiDnastics®: A Child-Centered Approach to Teaching Gymnastics* by Eric Malmberg, 2003, Champaign, IL: Human Kinetics.

Brachiation (Hand Over Hand)

From *KiDnastics®: A Child-Centered Approach to Teaching Gymnastics* by Eric Malmberg, 2003, Champaign, IL: Human Kinetics.

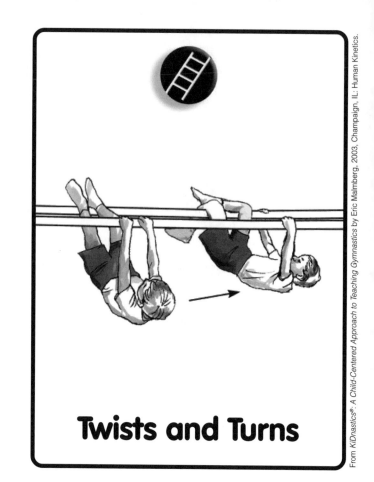

Twists and Turns

From *KiDnastics®: A Child-Centered Approach to Teaching Gymnastics* by Eric Malmberg, 2003, Champaign, IL: Human Kinetics.

Slanted Travel

From *KiDnastics®: A Child-Centered Approach to Teaching Gymnastics* by Eric Malmberg, 2003, Champaign, IL: Human Kinetics.

Pole or Rope Climb

From *KiDnastics®: A Child-Centered Approach to Teaching Gymnastics* by Eric Malmberg, 2003, Champaign, IL: Human Kinetics.

Rollover

Skin-the-Cat
Over and Back

From *KiDnastics®: A Child-Centered Approach to Teaching Gymnastics* by Eric Malmberg, 2003, Champaign, IL: Human Kinetics.

From *KiDnastics®: A Child-Centered Approach to Teaching Gymnastics* by Eric Malmberg, 2003, Champaign, IL: Human Kinetics.

Underswings

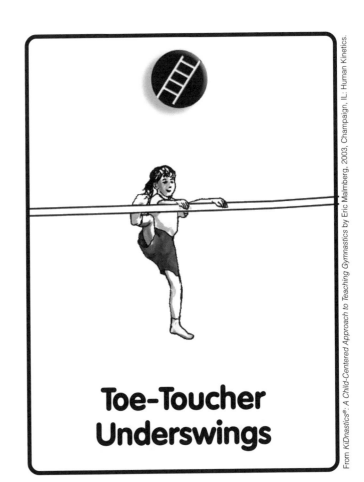

Toe-Toucher
Underswings

From *KiDnastics®: A Child-Centered Approach to Teaching Gymnastics* by Eric Malmberg, 2003, Champaign, IL: Human Kinetics.

From *KiDnastics®: A Child-Centered Approach to Teaching Gymnastics* by Eric Malmberg, 2003, Champaign, IL: Human Kinetics.

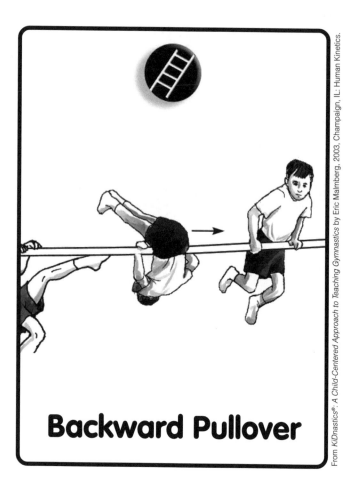

Backward Pullover

From *KiDnastics®: A Child-Centered Approach to Teaching Gymnastics* by Eric Malmberg, 2003, Champaign, IL: Human Kinetics.

Hand Support

From *KiDnastics®: A Child-Centered Approach to Teaching Gymnastics* by Eric Malmberg, 2003, Champaign, IL: Human Kinetics.

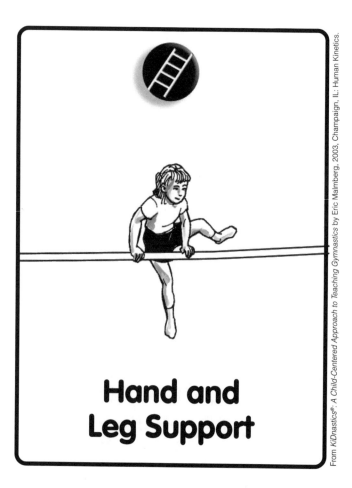

Hand and Leg Support

From *KiDnastics®: A Child-Centered Approach to Teaching Gymnastics* by Eric Malmberg, 2003, Champaign, IL: Human Kinetics.

Hip Casting

From *KiDnastics®: A Child-Centered Approach to Teaching Gymnastics* by Eric Malmberg, 2003, Champaign, IL: Human Kinetics.

About the Author

Eric Malmberg, EdD, has traveled the world studying gymnastics teaching and systems, and he has taught gymnastics at every level from preschool to national and Olympic levels. He has coached four national championship teams and numerous All-Americans, and he has been named National and Regional College Gymnastics Coach of the Year many times.

Malmberg is an associate professor of physical education and former department chair at the State University of New York at Cortland, where he was voted "most valuable faculty" by students in 2002. He has been a member of the USA Gymnastics Education Subcommittee for many years. He is also a member of the American Alliance for Health, Physical Education, Recreation and Dance; the National Association for Sport and Physical Education; the Council on Physical Education for Children; and the New York Alliance for Health, Physical Education, Recreation and Dance—the latter of which recently bestowed on him an Amazing Person Award. Malmberg is also coauthor of *Sequential Gymnastics* and *I Can Do Gymnastics*.

Malmberg holds a doctorate in teaching and curriculum from Syracuse University. He and his wife, Sue, live in Marathon, New York, and have three kids (who, according to Malmberg, constantly reinforce the principles brought forth in this book). In his leisure time, Malmberg enjoys hiking, kayaking, and backpacking.

What's the best way to build safe, effective and easy-to-manipulate KiDnastics® environments?

With genuine KiDnastics equipment from FlagHouse!

Developed in collaboration with accomplished gymnastics coach, physical educator, and author Dr. Eric Malmberg, each KiDnastics piece is:

- Versatile—appropriate for a variety of activities or combine with other KiDnastics pieces to create movement sequences and KiDnastic routines!

- Built to last—with top-quality materials that guarantee years of safe, reliable performance!

- Lightweight—easy to move and configure for instructors and students, alike!

**Get the maximum benefit from your movement education program—
Use genuine KiDnastics equipment available exclusively from FlagHouse!**

KiDnastics®
By **FLAGHOUSE**

Your complete source for physical education, fitness, sports, and recreation equipment.

Request a copy of our *Physical Education & Recreation* catalog to see the complete KiDnastics line—plus 8,000 more top-quality products!

FLAGHOUSE®
The Solutions You Need. The Source You Trust.

In the U.S.
800.793.7900
201.288.7600

In Canada
800.265.6900
416.495.8262

In Mexico
011.52.555.567.6484

www.FlagHouse.com